To Russ,
May this book
be an encouragement
to you. Praise God
for His faithfulness.

Janell

janell@mightbetuday.com

My Heart Will Always Cry

A Mother's Journey of Hope and
Healing for Her Hurting Heart

Janell Haworth Desmond

WestBow
PRESS
A DIVISION OF THOMAS NELSON

Scripture quotations taken from the Holy Bible, New Living Translation, copyright 1996, 2004. Used by permission of Tyndale House Publishers, Inc., Wheaton, Illinois 60189. All rights reserved.

WestBow Press books may be ordered through booksellers or by contacting:

WestBow Press
A Division of Thomas Nelson
1663 Liberty Drive
Bloomington, IN 47403
www.westbowpress.com
1-(866) 928-1240

Front cover photo and design by Julie Desmond

ISBN: 978-1-4497-1604-2 (sc)
ISBN: 978-1-4497-1605-9 (dj)
ISBN: 978-1-4497-1603-5 (e)

Library of Congress Control Number: 2011927131

Printed in the United States of America

WestBow Press rev. date: 04/19/2011

To God

*You alone are worthy of all
my praise and adoration.
May this book be used to glorify You.*

*"Weeping may last through the night,
but joy comes with the morning."*

Psalm 30:5b (NLT)

Acknowledgments

To my husband, Jim: Thank you for supporting me, even in my craziest ideas. You have always been there for me through the ups and downs of life. Thank you for holding me and letting me cry.

To my daughter, Julie: You are a blessing to me. Thank you for encouraging me and for helping me with this book. I couldn't have done it without you. Thank you for always listening to me as I talk things out.

To my family: Thanks for putting up with me all these years. I can always count on your love and support. Thank you especially for showing me the way to eternal life. Thank you for loving my son and walking beside me through all of the hard times.

I love you all very much.

Chapter 1

— ❦ —

My Heart Will Always Cry

There are a few days in my life that I can recall as if they happened yesterday. July 27, 1984 was such a day. The raw emotions, overwhelming feelings, and vivid details have never faded from my memory.

The chain of events leading up to this unforgettable day began earlier that year. My five-year-old son, Jeremy, was playing outside in the sandbox with his Tonka trucks, when a beautiful Siberian husky wandered into our yard. After a few days, we located the owners, and by the time they came to claim their pet, Jeremy had fallen in love. He decided he wanted a dog just like it.

Jeremy started doing chores around the house to earn money to buy a puppy. He collected aluminum cans from alongside the road to take to the local recycling center, where he would turn them in for cash. Once he even ended up with a bad case of poison oak from scrounging around for cans in a bushy patch of vegetation.

When Jeremy's sixth birthday rolled around in March, he requested money instead of toys so he would finally have enough to purchase the desired puppy. After doing research on dog breeds, we discovered an Alaskan malamute would be a better choice for a young child. Jeremy ended up buying an eight-week-old malamute pup.

Jeremy named his little ball of fluff Sheba. He loved her very much, and it was obvious that she was devoted to her young master. They ran and played until they were both exhausted. At night, Sheba would cuddle next to Jeremy as they slept in the warmth and comfort of his bed.

On July 27, 1984, Jeremy and six-month-old Sheba awoke to a seemingly normal day. It was a Saturday, and Jeremy and I drove down the mountain to Fresno to get groceries. We had tethered Sheba to a wire cable because we didn't have a fenced yard. While we were in Fresno, Sheba managed to free herself. When we got back home and pulled into the driveway, we saw her run to the other side of the road. Jeremy and I quickly got out of the car and crossed the street to bring her back home.

Before we had a chance to put a leash on her, she bolted into the road, just as a yellow Camaro sped around the corner. Jeremy yelled, "Stop, stop!" The driver of the Camaro didn't see her until it was too late. The impact threw her to the other side of the road. I held Jeremy's hand tightly as we ran back across the road to Sheba's side. We stood helplessly next to her as she tried to lift her weak and broken body, which moments earlier had been rambunctious and full of life. I will never forget the pleading look in her eyes as she gazed for the last time at the little boy she loved and trusted so much. Jeremy was overcome by emotion as the realization of what had just happened started to sink in. I had to physically restrain him so he wouldn't try to pick Sheba up.

The driver of the Camaro was an undercover policeman. He asked me to take Jeremy into the house and away from the painful scene of the accident. Jeremy was still hysterical, and as soon as we got inside the house, he threw himself on the floor. He began pounding it with his fists as he screamed, "No, no, no!"

I frantically grabbed the phonebook to find the number for a local veterinarian. I knew in my heart there was no hope, but I had to try to get help anyway, because my son was hurting. I couldn't just stand there and do nothing. I was still on the phone with the vet's office when my husband, Jim, came in and told us that Sheba had died.

Jim placed Sheba's body in a large black trash bag and dug a grave for her. He made a wooden cross and wrote Sheba's name and the date on it in orange paint. We had a graveside ceremony, and Jeremy placed the cross on the little mound of dirt and rocks that covered his beloved pet. Standing next to Sheba's grave, through tears of sorrow and pain, Jeremy expressed his deep love and profound loss by saying, "My heart will always cry for her."

All I could do was hold him and let him cry. He had just buried all of the hopes and dreams he had for the puppy he had worked for so lovingly. My heart ached for Jeremy, and I desperately wanted to take the pain away from him. This wouldn't be the last time in Jeremy's life that his hurt would be greater than my ability to console him.

Jeremy and Sheba

Chapter 2

———————— ❦ ————————

Back to the Beginning

My entrance into the world was actually quite eventful. I was born just twenty-one months after my sister, Jeanene. My mom had celebrated her twentieth birthday a week earlier, and my dad was only nineteen. I was born on the exact day I was due, October 4, 1953, in Roseville, California. My mom was very sick throughout the pregnancy. Then, during the birthing process, the umbilical cord bent, and I wasn't getting enough oxygen. The doctor quickly administered oxygen to my mom in an effort to keep me from suffocating. After some tense moments, my heart rate stabilized as my oxygen level increased. I was able to move around, and the cord straightened out. Thankfully, I survived the ordeal without any of the long-term physical effects that often plague babies born in an oxygen-deprived state.

I was taken to the nursery while my mom rested. After a few hours, she woke up and asked for her baby. A nurse went to get me. As my mom reached out her arms, she looked at the newborn and exclaimed, "This isn't my baby. My baby is prettier than that!" She was correct; they had brought a different baby. I'm glad she was paying attention, or who knows where I might have ended up!

The first memory I have is moving to a brand-new house in Orangevale, California, when I was three years old. My sister and I each had a cat. Jeanene got to take her cat, and I had to leave mine behind. I remember that when we drove up to the new house and opened the car door, Jeanene's cat jumped out and ran away. We never saw it again.

When I was four years old, I started kindergarten. I guess my stay-at-home mom missed me when I went to school, because my parents decided to have two more children, Leah and Laura. Later, when my mom was forty-four, daughter number five, Sarah, came along unexpectedly. Being the second of five daughters meant I wasn't the oldest, the youngest, or the middle child. I was simply "daughter number two."

I had a secure and family-oriented childhood. We moved throughout California every few years so my dad could climb the ladder in his career with the Federal Aviation Administration (FAA). We spent several summers in Oklahoma City while my dad attended FAA schooling. When we were there, we would travel ninety miles southeast to Ada, where my dad was born in 1934. He was an only child and still owned his family's original eighty-acre homestead just outside of town. His family had left Ada in March of 1942, when times got tough in Oklahoma. They packed everything they owned into their Model A and headed to the promised land of California. They settled in Northern California and found work in the orchards. My granddaddy was eventually hired by the railroad in Roseville.

My mother was a California native. Her dad also worked for the railroad in Roseville, until he died from alcohol abuse when he was in his fifties.

While I was growing up, I was mostly compliant and easygoing. But sometimes I could be a little rascal. In second grade, if we got a perfect score on our math papers, we would get a piece of candy. I was fairly good at math, but I wanted that candy so much that I had my best friend Pam, who was really good at math, do the problems for me. It was working well until Pam accidently wrote her name on my paper. She erased it and wrote my name, but the teacher still caught it. My parents were called in, and I was very embarrassed, not to mention in big trouble.

In third grade, I tried to stay out of trouble, but sometimes I couldn't help myself. In those days, girls had to wear dresses to school. I loved to play on the monkey bars, and according to my parents, full and frilly dresses were not appropriate for turning upside down and around and around while hanging from a bar.

One day, I deliberately disobeyed my parents and wore a pair of shorts under my dress so I could play on the monkey bars. When recess time came, I was happily twirling around on the bars when I accidentally caught my hand on a ruffle and tore my dress! I started to feel sick to my stomach, because I wasn't sure what I was going to tell my parents when they saw my dress.

I took my time walking home from school. As I came through the front door, my mom immediately saw the tear.

"Jan, it looks like your dress has been ripped. How did that happen?" she asked.

I didn't want her to know I had disobeyed, so I thought fast. "Eddie ran by me on my way home from school and grabbed my dress and it tore," I lied.

She became noticeably upset and replied, "When your dad gets home from work, you can tell him what Eddie did, and he will know what to do about it."

The sick feeling in the pit of my stomach only got worse. It seemed like my dad would never get home. I didn't really want him to come home, because I would have to retell my lie and hope he didn't try to call or go over to Eddie's house and tell his parents about it.

When he finally got home, my mom told me to tell him what had happened to my dress. I repeated my lie. "I was walking home from school, and Eddie ran by and tore my dress."

My dad didn't miss a beat as he proceeded to tell me a story about when he was a little boy. "One day, a neighbor girl told her mother I had torn her dress at school," he said. "That night, the mother and daughter came to my house and falsely accused me. I told them that I had not torn her dress and that it must have been someone else. The girl was standing behind her mother, and at that point she started to cry. Between sobs, she admitted she had torn it doing something she was not supposed to be doing." Then my dad looked me straight in the eye and said, "Do you want to come with me to Eddie's house and tell his parents that he tore your dress?"

I started crying and told him the truth about how I tore my dress. I don't know to this day if he really had the same experience or if he just made up his story to get me to confess. I hated admitting my lie, but at the same time, I felt relieved to be back in a good and open relationship with my parents.

Janell and Jeanene - May 1958

Chapter 3

— ❦ —

Things Were Looking Up

From as early as I can remember, my family attended church every time the doors were open. When I was eight years old, our church hosted a week of revival meetings. Since I had attended church and Sunday school my whole life, I had heard about God's love for me and how He had sent His Son, Jesus, to earth to die for our sins. I believed that, but for some reason I had never realized that I was born a sinner and needed to confess my sins to God and ask Him to come into my life. During the revival, it was as if my eyes had been opened, and I desperately wanted to belong to God's family. I knew what I needed to do. I needed to pray. Each night when I got into bed, I prayed and asked God to forgive my sins and come into my life. I'm not sure what I expected to happen, but I wasn't convinced God had heard my prayer. I vividly recall praying night after night that God would forgive my sins and save me.

On the final night of the revival, I called my mom into my room and said, "Mom, I have been praying and asking God to forgive my sins. But I'm not sure if it really happened. I want to be a Christian. I just keep praying for it every night."

My mom took my hand as she said to me, "Jan, if you truly believe, go ahead and pray out loud right now. I know God is listening."

I bowed my head and prayed, "Dear God, thank You for sending Your Son, Jesus, to die on the cross for me. I know I am a sinner. Please forgive me. I want to live for You from now on. Amen."

My mom hugged me and said, "Now you are a Christian. God always hears the prayer of one asking to become part of His family. God will never leave you. He will help you with everything in your life. Now you will go to heaven when you die and live with Him forever."

I felt so much joy at that moment. It wasn't until just a few years ago that I finally understood why I had prayed so many times and never felt like I was truly saved. I was reading the verse in the Bible that says, "For if you confess with your mouth that Jesus is Lord and believe in your heart that God raised Him from the dead, you will be saved. For it is by believing in your heart that you are made right with God, and it is by confessing with your mouth that you are saved" (Romans 10:9-10 NLT).

I think what I needed was to share with someone what had happened in my heart with an outward declaration of what had taken place inside me. Since that night, I have never doubted that God is with me and loves me unconditionally.

Chapter 4

——————— ❧ ———————

'60s and '70s

Growing up in the '60s and '70s proved to be an interesting experience. I remember the first time I saw a color television set. It belonged to a wealthy family in our neighborhood, and it seemed unlikely we would ever have enough money to own one.

I remember milk being delivered to our front porch in glass bottles. Sometimes my mom ordered chocolate milk as a special treat. The Fuller Brush man and the Avon lady came to our house to sell products to my mom. I loved it when the Avon lady gave me one of her lipstick samples in a small white tube.

I clearly remember a defining event of the '60s that happened as I sat in my fifth-grade classroom. On November 22, 1963, I listened as an announcement came over the intercom. President John F. Kennedy had been shot and killed in Dallas. The teacher was very upset. My mom heard the news on the radio, and when I got home from school, she was still crying. The country was devastated. Everyone loved JFK.

During the late '60s, Jeanene and I wore bell bottoms and mini-skirts. My parents bought us a Beatles record. Guys I knew were being drafted into the Vietnam War. I thought I was being so cool when I flashed a peace sign at someone.

I was very social, never lacked for friends, and always had a boyfriend or two. I guess that is what led the junior high counselor to note in my permanent school record, "Janell is very flighty."

I survived the '60s and graduated from John F. Kennedy High School in Fremont, California, in 1971. After high school, I attended Multnomah Bible College in Portland, Oregon, for three years. I finished my bachelor's degree in education at The Master's College in 1975 and began teaching at a Christian school in Southern California.

Chapter 5

───────── ❦ ─────────

Big Changes

During the summer of 1976, when the youth from our church went to camp, I volunteered to go along as their counselor. Finding a boyfriend was the furthest thing from my mind that week. I wasn't expecting the camp speaker to take an interest in me. Nick wanted to become a youth pastor and was spending his summer speaking for various youth camps. We started dating, even though we lived an hour away from each other.

That fall, Nick accepted a position as a youth pastor at a church near my home. It seemed like things were falling into place for us, and I thought our relationship would become permanent. Nick took me to look at new condominiums with him, and when we were around other people, he would say things like, "What do you think of my girl?" We spent time together on a regular basis for the next ten months but he never told me he loved me.

Then one morning, I woke up feeling nauseated. I tried to eat some breakfast, but I couldn't keep it down. I thought I was just tired from getting up early to attend graduate summer school courses at Cal State Northridge and waitressing at Bob's Big Boy late into the night. But as I thought about it, I realized my period was overdue. I started to feel even sicker to my stomach.

I was frightened by the possibility that I might be pregnant. Even though I had a very active dating life, I had determined to remain a virgin until I married. That all changed when I met Nick. Nick's strong, charismatic confidence, good build, and curly light-brown hair made him hard to resist.

Back in 1977, we did not have home pregnancy tests readily available at drug stores, gas stations, and even the dollar stores, like we do now. I knew I would have to see a doctor to confirm whether or not I was pregnant. My health coverage was with Kaiser-Permanente in Panorama City. Since I had been planning to go to Anaheim and visit some friends that weekend, I scheduled an appointment for a pregnancy test that Friday. After I saw the doctor and gave a urine sample, the nurse told me she would call me with the results on Monday. I asked if I could contact her instead, because I didn't want my mom to answer the phone. She said I could call first thing Monday morning. I spent the weekend at Disneyland with my friends, even though I didn't feel like it was the happiest place on Earth right then.

When Monday finally came, I went upstairs and used the phone in my parents' room to call the doctor's office. The nurse confirmed that I was pregnant.

I was terrified of telling my parents. I felt sicker and sicker by the hour. The one thing I did not want to do was to embarrass them. I knew how happy they were over the late-in-life baby they were expecting, and I didn't want to put a damper on their excitement.

By Wednesday, I knew I had to tell them, and I decided to do so in a letter. I just couldn't face them. I composed the letter that afternoon and then called my fifteen-year-old sister, Laura, upstairs and confided in her that I was pregnant. She was the first person I told. I asked her to give the letter to my parents when they got home from church that night. Then I went to work, all the while knowing what I had to face when my shift ended. However, I felt so sick from nerves that I had to leave work early.

When I walked into the house, it was obvious that Laura had given them the letter. They were both sitting in the living room, crying. The emotions were so overwhelming that I don't remember what was said. I went upstairs and cried myself to sleep.

Nick was out of town that week, and when he got back Saturday night, I called him and told him I really needed to see him the next day. We met at a local Chinese restaurant, and as he ate lunch, I told him I was pregnant. He indicated that he did not want to marry me and even suggested that I have an abortion. I told him we only had two choices: we could either get married or not get married. I would keep the baby, whether he married me or not. Abortion was never a consideration on my part.

I saw Nick a couple more times during the early part of my pregnancy, before he stopped calling altogether.

In January of 1978, my family moved to Fresno. My mom had just given birth to my little sister, Sarah. Since my doctor was still in Southern California, I moved in with my newly married sister, Jeanene, and her husband, Darrel, so I could be closer to the hospital. They lived in Rosamond, which was still about an hour and a half away from the hospital.

During the '70s, natural childbirth was very popular. I didn't want to use any drugs during the labor or delivery and chose to follow the Bradley Method of natural childbirth. I asked Jeanene to be my birthing coach, and we attended a series of classes prior to the birth. At that time, ultrasounds weren't common unless there was a problem with the pregnancy. Since I had no complications, I never had an ultrasound, and I didn't know if I would have a boy or a girl.

I went to church with Jeanene and Darrel on Palm Sunday, March 19, 1978. It was three days past my official due date. During the church service, I started having contractions about every five minutes, but I felt no pain whatsoever. I took a nap after lunch and then went for a walk. The painless contractions continued all day. Around nine o'clock that night, the contractions became a little more intense but still not painful. We decided to go to the hospital just in case.

Laura was on spring break and had come to stay with us in Rosamond for the week. Jeanene took me to the hospital in her little yellow Spitfire, and Laura squeezed into the back, behind the seat. When we got to the hospital at 10:30 p.m., the nurse said I was dilated to eight centimeters. She broke my water, and I immediately had an overwhelming urge to push. The doctor on duty was busy delivering another baby, so the nurse told me not to push, and she left the room. Resisting the urge to push was easier said than done!

Jeanene was in the labor room with me as I did deep breathing and tried desperately not to push. After a while, Jeanene checked to see if she could see the baby coming. She told me that she saw the baby's head starting to emerge and that it had quite a bit of brown hair. She called the nurse back into the room. The nurse took one look and asked my sister to leave. I told the nurse that Jeanene was my coach and I needed her. She informed me that only husbands were allowed in the delivery room. That was a fine time to tell us! I was very upset at this news, but we couldn't do anything about it at that point. As I watched Jeanene walk out the door, I felt very alone.

The nurse hastily wheeled me into a surgery room, because all of the delivery rooms were full. Moments later, the doctor dashed in. He quickly put on gloves and checked my progress. He told me to push with the next contraction. I pushed once, and literally out popped my baby. The nurse looked at the clock and said, "1:23 a.m. It's a boy." I quietly said to myself, "That's Jeremy David." I had been at the hospital less than three hours. Jeremy was born on March 20, 1978. It was the first day of spring.

As soon as the cord was cut they placed my eight-pound baby boy in an incubator. He was crying, and I desperately wanted to hold him. The quick delivery had caused a lot of tearing, and it took the doctor forty-five minutes to stitch me up. When they finally handed Jeremy to me, I started feeling pretty inadequate for what was ahead. I now had this adorable baby boy depending on me for everything. Despite my fears, tears of joy streamed down my face as I held my precious baby boy in my arms for the first time and thought, *What did I ever do without him?* I loved him so much. He was perfect. I knew that I had made a mistake, but I also knew that God does not make mistakes, and this life was a miracle and a gift from Him.

We stayed with Jeanene and Darrel for the first four weeks of Jeremy's life. Then Jeremy and I moved in with my parents in Fresno. Even though my mom had a new baby of her own, they helped me all they could. I got a job as a directory assistance operator for Pacific Telephone. With child care, rent, and other expenses, I struggled to make it from paycheck to paycheck.

I had not been in contact with Nick since the first trimester of my pregnancy, and I decided not to ask him for any financial help. His dad had died six years earlier, leaving him with several small businesses to run. Nick had managed them poorly, and he eventually went bankrupt (yet somehow he was still able to drive a Mercedes). He didn't want anything to do with me or Jeremy personally, so I decided to keep him out of our lives financially as well. Mutual friends told him that I had a boy. They also told me Nick was off somewhere with another woman the weekend Jeremy was born.

Chapter 6

———————— ❦ ————————

Encounter at McDonald's

On the Sunday mornings that I didn't have to work, Jeremy and I attended Fresno Evangelical Free Church. When Jeremy was three months old, I decided to have him dedicated to the Lord during the worship service. This public dedication was my promise to the Lord that I would do everything within my power to raise him in a godly way. I was praying that when he was old enough, he would make his own personal decision to follow God.

The weekend I had Jeremy dedicated, Jeanene and Darrel were camping at Lake Kaweah, near Three Rivers, California. The campground was less than two hours from Fresno, and Darrel brought Jeanene over on Saturday so she could stay with me and attend the service. We drove back to the lake on Sunday afternoon.

A few weeks before the dedication, I attended a social event sponsored by the singles department of the church. That night, I met a girl who worked for a Christian camp located 65 miles from Fresno. During our conversation, we realized that we both knew Nick, but I didn't mention he was my baby's biological father. She told me he and his youth group would be attending camp in a few weeks. I didn't know what church he was working for at that time and didn't give it any more thought.

After the baby dedication, Leah, Laura, Jeanene, Jeremy, and I started driving toward Lake Kaweah. We stopped for lunch in Visalia but couldn't decide between Taco Bell and McDonald's. Laura and I said we would rather go to McDonald's. Jeanene, who was driving my red Dodge Colt wagon, proceeded to the drive-thru so we wouldn't have to take Jeremy out of his car seat.

After we got our order and started to drive away, I looked up and saw a church bus pulling into the parking lot. I glanced at the bus driver and realized it was Nick. I told my sisters how the girl at church had told me he would be taking his youth group to camp. Jeanene circled around and stopped in front of the bus. I immediately realized it was no coincidence that we were coming from Fresno and he was coming from Southern California and just happened to end up in Visalia at the same McDonald's at the same time.

I sat in the car, trembling with fear, as we waited for all of the kids to get off the bus. Nick was still in the driver's seat, rubbing his eyes as I got Jeremy out of his car seat. I carried Jeremy to the bottom of the steps just as Nick was exiting the bus. When he saw us, it was obvious he was extremely shocked and therefore speechless. When he finally spoke, he just kept saying that Jeremy was so cute. Then he said we should start seeing each other again and asked me to call him when I was in Southern California.

We saw him twice after that. The third time I called to let him know we were coming down, he told me he had changed his mind. He said if he ever really felt like getting back together with me, it would probably be too late, because I would likely be with someone else. Since it seemed we had no future together, I told him if he ever married, he needed to make sure his wife knew about Jeremy, because I would not keep Jeremy from meeting him one day if Jeremy wanted to.

I had been on an emotional roller coaster with Nick for the past few months, and I knew I couldn't go on like that any longer. It was time for me to get on with my life and put Nick in my past.

Jeremy David

Chapter 7

———— ❦ ————

Who Are You and What Do You Do?

On Friday, December 29, 1978, I got down on my knees and asked God to forgive me for my past mistakes. I knew that God was loving and forgiving. The Bible says if we confess our sins to God, He will forgive us and cleanse us from every wrong thing we have done (I John 1:9). After asking for forgiveness, I asked God to provide me with a husband and a daddy for Jeremy.

I remember thinking that I would probably have to wait awhile before God would bring someone to us. I didn't expect an immediate answer to my prayer. But this time I guess God was just waiting for my heart to be ready. Two days after praying that prayer, I met a man in the singles Sunday school class I had been attending. I had never seen him there before, even though he had been coming to the class off and on for several months. Until that day, our work schedules had prevented us from being there on the same Sunday. He started talking about organizing a cross-country-skiing trip for the class in the nearby mountains.

Finally I said, "Who are you and what do you do?"

"My name is Jim Desmond, and I work for the US Forest Service," he answered.

When class ended, we continued to talk as we made our way to the sanctuary, where we sat next to one another. After the service was over, it seemed like we kept getting pushed together as we exited the crowded sanctuary. Finally, to my surprise, Jim asked if I would go out to lunch with him that afternoon. I told him I thought I could arrange for my mom to watch Jeremy. He knew I had a son because I had shared with the class that my baby had been very sick just a week earlier on Christmas Day.

I drew a quick map on the back of the church bulletin, showing Jim how to get to my parents' house. He picked me up an hour later and we went to eat at Marie Callender's restaurant for our first date.

One of the things that attracted me to Jim was that it was easy to talk to him. I felt comfortable around him from the start. As we ate our prime rib dinner, he shared with me that he was born in Muncie, Indiana. When he was twelve years old, his family moved to San Diego. We discovered that our paths almost crossed years earlier when we had both gone to see President Kennedy on his visit to San Diego in 1963. I was nine and Jim was sixteen at the time.

Jim graduated from Hoover High School in San Diego and then attended San Diego City College before transferring to Humboldt State in Arcata, California. He had planned to become a coach and teach biology. After graduating from Humboldt, he continued on to graduate school at Chico State, which was a well-known party school at that time. Jim took advantage of the party life, attending as many keggers as possible. That lifestyle eventually caught up with him, and he received a letter from the school, telling him he was no longer welcome to attend, as his grade-point average had dropped below an acceptable level. Once Jim had flunked out of graduate school and teaching was no longer an option, he started seeking other types of employment.

Jim eventually got a job with the US Forest Service in Quincy, a very small town in Northern California. During the time he worked there, his life changed dramatically.

There wasn't much for a single person to do in Quincy, so some of Jim's co-workers had introduced him to gambling in nearby Reno, Nevada. Jim had started going to Reno to gamble on his days off.

Jim had another co-worker named Ral, who was also the youth leader at the First Baptist Church in Quincy. Ral invited Jim over to his house on several occasions to meet with other young adults for food and fellowship. Jim was glad to go, because he was hoping to meet some cute girls. What he didn't know was that God had plans for his life way beyond meeting girls.

One Sunday night during one of these get-togethers, Ral gave a short message on the topic of sin. Ral told them sin wasn't just stealing, murder, or adultery, but also things like pride, selfishness, and living a life separated from God. Jim spoke up and asked if gambling was a sin. Ral simply replied, "Why don't you ask God to tell you if gambling is a sin or not." Jim thought that sounded like a challenge in which he could put God to the test. He was off the next day and had planned to go to Reno to gamble.

On his way to Reno Jim said, "God, if you are real and if gambling is a sin, show me."

He walked into Diamond Jim's Nevada Club on that Monday morning and bought his chips to play blackjack. He was pretty good at the game and usually won some money. In order to win at blackjack, the player has to have a higher card value than the dealer but cannot go over twenty-one. Jim was dealt excellent hands that totaled nineteen or twenty each time. Hand after hand, the dealer always scored one point better. Jim didn't win once. He couldn't believe it! That had never happened to him before. He kept playing until he lost all of the money he had allocated for gambling that day.

As he stood up from the table in shock and disbelief, he heard an inner voice speaking to him. He immediately knew it was God saying that He was indeed real, and He wanted Jim to believe in Him. Jim had challenged God to reveal Himself, and God had done just that. Jim smiled as he realized he had played blackjack against God that day, and God had won his heart.

As he quickly walked out of the casino, Jim suddenly became very aware of the evil all around him. But inside he felt new and clean as he prayed and told God that he believed He was real and he needed Him in his life.

When he got back to Quincy, he went to Ral's house and shared with him how God had answered his prayer and how he had surrendered his life to Jesus Christ in the middle of a casino in Reno, Nevada. The next Sunday was Easter, and Jim was baptized. He was twenty-four years old at the time.

Jim spent the next seven years in Quincy. When he was thirty-one years old, he transferred to Shaver Lake, California, with the US Forest Service and started attending Fresno Evangelical Free Church, where we met.

We were married On April 28, 1979, just sixteen weeks after we met. My prayer had been answered. God gave me a man who loved me, and Jeremy had a daddy! Jim and Jeremy had fallen in love as quickly as Jim and I.

Our wedding ceremony was held in my parents' backyard on a perfect spring afternoon. After we exchanged our vows, my aunt Marilyn went to the piano and started playing, "Jesus Loves the Little Children." As she played, my dad handed thirteen-month-old Jeremy to Jim. Jeremy reached out to Jim with his little arms and said, "Papa."

Then Jim said vows to Jeremy. "Just as I took Janell to be my wife, I take Jeremy to be my son." He looked at Jeremy and said, "I promise to provide for you in every way possible, to give you a loving Christian home, an education, all that you need, and especially the love of a father." There wasn't a dry eye in the house! At the end of the ceremony, the three of us walked down the aisle as a family for the first time.

An outdoor reception immediately followed the ceremony, and some unusual guests showed up. Several of Jim's co-workers were in the annual Clovis Rodeo Parade that day, not far from my parents' home. After the parade, they decided to crash our wedding reception. The kids were thrilled when Smokey Bear and Woodsy Owl walked into the backyard and started passing out balloons. I doubt if very many people can say they had a giant bear and huge owl as guests at their wedding reception!

Jeanene and Darrel were happy to watch Jeremy as we honeymooned along the California coast for a week. Then we settled into a small US Forest Service-owned single-wide trailer in Big Creek, California. My life had changed dramatically in a short amount of time.

*Jim, Woodsy Owl, Smokey Bear, Jeremy and Janell
at our wedding reception - April 28, 1979.*

Chapter 8

———— ❧ ————

Adoption

A couple of weeks before our wedding, Nick had called out of the blue. Before he had the chance to say anything, I told him I was engaged to be married. Nick asked me if Jim loved me, and I told him he did. I informed him that Jim was planning to adopt Jeremy as soon as he could.

Nick replied, "No problem. Just send me the paperwork." Later, when he received it, he immediately signed and sent it back.

Jeremy was too young to remember ever meeting Nick, and if we hadn't told him differently, he would have thought Jim was his biological father. The social worker assigned to our case suggested we tell two-year-old Jeremy about the adoption in a way he could understand. I told Jeremy that Nick didn't have a job (which was true at the time) and he couldn't take care of us. I told him that his papa had come along and loved us both very much and wanted to be his daddy.

I remember the day we went to the courthouse in Fresno and into the judge's chambers. Jeremy was on the floor behind the judge's big oak desk, playing with a little red Hot Wheels fire truck. Just as the judge said, "Jeremy David Haworth shall now be named Jeremy David Desmond," Jeremy popped up and said, "That's me."

When we told Jeremy about Nick, we were careful not to say anything negative about him. Even so, one day soon after the adoption,

I was making my bed, and Jeremy was playing with some toys on the floor when he suddenly said, "Why didn't Nick love me?" I told him that Nick didn't know him, and if he did, he would surely have loved him.

Jim and Jeremy - March 1980

Chapter 9

⯌

Where's My Brother?

After a year of marriage, we decided we wanted to have another child. In planning the pregnancy, we had to take into account Jim's job as a wildland firefighter and the May-through-October California fire season. Having a baby in the middle of winter wasn't a good idea for us either because of the snowy conditions in which we lived. Our planning paid off, and right on schedule I became pregnant. We anxiously awaited the arrival of our new baby sometime in March of 1981.

Jim's mom and dad were excited about having another grandchild and were ready to come as soon as they got the word that I was in labor. However, a few days before the baby was due, we received a phone call in the early morning hours. It was Jim's sister-in-law, Gloria, calling to tell us that his mom had a heart attack and was taken to the local hospital in Watsonville. The phone call came as a surprise, since Jim's mom was only sixty-seven years old and in seemingly good health.

We immediately packed our things and drove down the mountain. We left Jeremy with my parents in Clovis before heading for the coast.

When we got to Watsonville, we drove straight to Jim's parents' house. As we stepped into the living room, we saw Jim's brother and sister-in-law sitting next to each other on the couch. His dad sat quietly in his favorite leather recliner and seemed somewhat distracted and confused. We didn't immediately realize that Jim's mom had died and were wondering why no one was with her at the hospital. Finally, Jim's brother, John, started talking about the initial heart attack and then the massive fatal heart attack that had happened during an angiogram the doctor had ordered.

I called Jeremy to tell him that Grandma Helen had died. He got mad and kept saying, "No, no, she's not dead." He was about to turn three years old, yet even at that young age, he understood the impact of what I had told him.

We held a memorial service for her at Jim's parents' church in Watsonville and then drove back home. Since the baby could come at any time, and there was still snow in the Sierra Nevadas, we stayed with my parents so we would be near the hospital. Jim commuted up the mountain to work.

We celebrated Jeremy's third birthday with a party on Saturday, March 21. My mom made a green Oscar the Grouch cake at Jeremy's request. The next morning, Jim got up and drove to the Shaver Lake Ranger Station. Not long after he left my parents' house, I felt some discomfort in my back. I stayed home from church, because it had become difficult to sit down for very long. My parents took Jeremy to the early service, and my sister Leah stayed home with me. I began having discharge that indicated the baby was probably ready to come. I called Jim at his office. He had just arrived and was getting ready to go out into the forest for the day. I was lucky to catch him in time. He immediately drove the hour back down the mountain.

Jim picked me up, and we made a dash for Fresno Community Hospital. We arrived at the hospital emergency entrance at 10 a.m. They quickly wheeled me into a labor room, and the midwife checked my progress. She said that the birth was imminent.

Jim held my hand as the baby was born forty-two minutes after we arrived at the hospital. Jim was very excited, and the first thing he said was, "It's a little girl! It's a little girl!" The midwife immediately handed my baby girl to me as Jim cut the cord.

I called my parents' house just as they had returned from church. I asked to speak to Jeremy first.

"Jeremy, you have a baby sister," I said.

"Yea!" he said. "Where's my brother?"

I realized later that when we kept telling him he would have a baby brother or sister, he thought he would have a baby brother *and* sister.

We named our little six-pound-two-ounce baby girl Julie. We were able to take her home from the hospital the same day she was born, and she slept peacefully through the first night.

Chapter 10

---- ❦ ----

Good Times

When Julie was five weeks old, we moved out of the small two-bedroom rental house we had been living in for the last year in Big Creek, to a new double-wide mobile home we had purchased. The mobile home was set up forty-five minutes down the mountain from Big Creek at the Mountain Rest fire station on Old Tollhouse Road. This put us closer to Fresno and near the top of Highway 168. We would live at Mountain Rest for the next seven years.

During those seven years, the kids loved playing outside together and were privileged to have the beautiful mountains of the Sierra Nevada as their playground. We lived an hour from the Sierra Summit ski area, and during the winter, the school would take the students there for skiing lessons. Jeremy and Julie were also able to walk outside our door and sled down the hill toward the fire station. I would watch them from the comfort of our warm house. When they needed a break from the snow and cold, they would come in for hot chocolate, and I would throw their wet clothes in the dryer. Once their snowsuits were dry and they had warmed up, they would head back out to play in the beautiful winter wonderland.

One of Julie's favorite winter activities was ice skating. She had learned to skate at an indoor rink in Fresno and even took lessons one summer. She loved watching skating competitions on television, and when the Ice Capades came to Fresno, she couldn't wait to see the show. The highlight of each winter for Julie was when we took her to ice skate on the outdoor rink in Yosemite Valley. Julie couldn't have been happier, doing her favorite thing in such a beautiful setting.

Jeremy loved nature and enjoyed exploring, hiking, and fishing. Jim took Jeremy with him on several tree-planting projects, which instilled a lifelong love for trees within him. He planted trees in our yard everywhere we lived. Our tradition for many Christmases was to buy a living Christmas tree and then plant it in the yard after the holidays. The last year we did this was 1998, and the tree now stands over twelve feet tall.

Even though we have a lot of fond memories of our life at Mountain Rest, it was not without drama. Besides the tragic death of Sheba, one Saturday morning in September of 1987, we all had a pretty big scare.

Jeremy and Julie both had friends sleep over on Friday night. All four kids were up early and had gone outside to play while I fixed breakfast. Since it was still fire season, Jim had already left for work. Julie and Chelsea were painting rocks with watercolors on the picnic table, while Jeremy and Michael were playing with their BB guns. The girls didn't know where the boys were until they heard some noise in a nearby tree and went over to investigate. When they realized it was just the boys, they headed back toward the table. The next thing Julie remembers is looking down as blood began to run down her leg.

Suddenly Chelsea burst through the front door and told me Julie had been shot with a BB. I ran to the front porch as Julie limped up the steps. Jeremy and Michael were just climbing down from the tree. I have to admit I became a little hysterical as I approached Jeremy, grabbed his BB gun, and threw it to the ground. I asked what happened, and Jeremy said he had accidentally shot Julie. Julie said she heard one of the boys say, "Let's shoot at their feet."

Whether the shot was intentional or not did not concern me at that moment. My concern was whether the bullet had actually gone into Julie's leg or bounced off. I had her sit on the steps and hold a washcloth over the site of the bullet wound.

I went inside and called a twenty-four-hour dial-a-nurse help line. I attempted to describe the situation to the nurse. She told me to take some deep breaths and calm down. She said that the bullet could have penetrated a quarter inch or so into Julie's leg and that I should have a doctor look at it right away.

Since it was Saturday and the doctors' offices were closed, I took Julie down to the emergency room at Valley Children's Hospital. Chelsea and Michael's mothers picked them up before we started down the four-lane highway toward Fresno. When we arrived at the hospital, they took X-rays of Julie's leg and discovered that the BB had gone all the way into the leg and lodged in her bone. The doctor told me they would leave the BB in her leg, since trying to get it out would be dangerous. He said the BB had entered at such a high speed, there was no fear of infection setting in, and Julie should be fine.

A police report had to be entered, since the incident involved a firearm. We were not allowed to leave the hospital until an officer arrived and interviewed Jeremy. Julie was sure they were going to arrest her nine-year-old brother on the spot. Jeremy was pretty scared, and when we got home, I took the BB gun and told Jeremy he couldn't have it back until he turned twelve.

The last scary incident we had while living at Mountain Rest happened in 1988 on Easter Sunday morning. Jeremy had a dog named Samantha at the time. We had tied Sam up with a rope bolted into the ground so she would stay in the yard. Sam's barking awakened me at 4 a.m. and I got up and peeked out of the curtains in the living room. Sam had forcefully pulled so hard on the rope that the bolt came right out of the ground. She was standing behind the car, barking as if her life depended on it. I quickly realized that her life did depend on it and she was barking at a large mountain lion that was pacing back and forth just twelve feet away from her. I ran to the door and opened it. Sam made a mad dash for the house, and the mountain lion fled across the street. Sam raced down the hallway and jumped into bed with Jim. He was startled to be awakened so suddenly by this shaking and frightened canine. Needless to say, we didn't go back to sleep.

A few weeks later, we had our mobile home moved to Auberry, where we would live for the next five years. We knew Auberry well because we were all actively involved in Auberry Community Church. Jim and I taught the junior high group and frequently sponsored youth activities. We were active in a weekly AWANA Bible Club at the church. I led the music, Jeremy helped out with recreation for the younger kids, and Julie was a member of the club. Jeremy participated in many activities and attended summer church camp on several occasions. During his spring break in 1993, he went on a mission trip to Mexico. He was an instant hit with the kids they went to help and felt a genuine love and compassion for them.

Jeremy also kept busy with extracurricular activities at school. When he was in fifth grade, he played the lead in *Tom Sawyer*. He was an exceptional actor and stole the show. He sang in the school chorus and didn't mind it at all that he was the only boy in the group. I think maybe he even preferred it that way. He was so outgoing and popular that he was chosen as the boy with the best personality in his eighth-grade class.

We had fond memories of the years we spent in the mountains and foothills above Fresno. But unfortunately, as all good things do, our time in that community came to an end.

Jeremy (5) and Julie (2) playing outside our home at Mountain Rest

Chapter 11

Moving On

When my dad retired from the FAA in 1989, he, my mom, and Sarah moved from California to Oklahoma. He began building a house on the eighty acres he still owned in Ada. A few years earlier, both Jeanene and Laura and their families had moved to Ozark, Arkansas. Leah and her family remained in Fresno.

Not long after Jim's mom died, his dad, whom we called Grandpa Ray, moved closer to us so he could be more involved with the kids. He moved into a senior citizens' mobile home park a few miles from us. At the age of eighty-one, Grandpa Ray married seventy-nine-year-old Rosie, his next-door neighbor. Three years later, on April 15, 1993, Grandpa Ray died. Dying on tax day was ironic for him, because one of his favorite sayings was, "Only two things in life are certain: death and taxes." After Grandpa Ray died, we decided to leave the area.

I was employed at Auberry School, teaching special-education students. Jim was still working for the US Forest Service. We began praying about where God would have us move. Jim applied for many promotions within the federal government, without success. Then in September of 1993, he was finally offered a position with the National Park Service in Van Buren, Missouri. Jim became the fire management officer for Ozark National Scenic Riverways, which is a river park on the Current River. The town of Van Buren is located in the Ozarks, with a population of less than a thousand. Van Buren was an ideal location as it was five and a half hours from Jeanene and Laura in Arkansas and seven and a half hours from my parents and Sarah in Oklahoma.

We moved to Van Buren when Jeremy was fifteen and Julie was twelve. Jim's report date was in October, so he and Julie went on ahead a month before Jeremy and me. We stayed in California to let Jeremy finish the football season, since we already knew the school he would be going to was too small to have a football team. He played defensive end for the junior varsity team at Sierra High School. Jeremy was a disciplined player and a natural leader. He gave 100 percent, even during the hot and grueling practice sessions. I attended and videotaped every game. I would only turn the recorder on when he was on the field. Therefore, our video clips only feature jersey number 75 and the announcer's voice saying, "Desmond on the play."

In late November, Jeremy played his final high school football game and attended his last dance with many of the kids he had known since he was three years old. I picked him up when the dance was over, and we drove to my sister Leah and her husband Zeke's house in Fresno to spend the night. We slept a few hours and then began our journey to Missouri. Our blue Mazda sedan was loaded with last-minute things, as well as two parakeets named Carney and Tootsie. Jeremy had to give his tropical fish away because they would have been too hard to transport.

Neither Jeremy nor I realized the impact driving away from our home would have on us. For several years, we had talked about moving, and Jeremy had always loved going back to Oklahoma and Arkansas to stay with family during the summer. He had started spending his summers there when he was nine and had made many friends. But the reality of playing his last football game and going to the dance with friends he may never see again hit him hard. He barely spoke the entire trip. I began to think about how difficult it must be for Jeremy to leave behind everything he had known. I replayed in my mind many of the events of the last fifteen years.

Chapter 12

— ❦ —

Looking Back

We recognized early on that Jeremy was a very headstrong and determined child. However, as with most strong-willed children, he responded well to discipline. He needed structure and to know what we expected of him. When he was three years old, I was reading a book by James Dobson called *Dare to Discipline.* Jeremy heard me talking to Jim concerning some of the things I had learned from the book about disciplining children. After a while, I noticed Jeremy had quietly disappeared from the living room, so I went to check on him. I found him in the bathroom looking down at my copy of the book, which was now soaking in the toilet!

As a young boy, Jeremy had two speeds: full-bore or crash. Before he started kindergarten, I was afraid he would have a hard time sitting still in class because he was such an active child. As it turned out, Jeremy was a model student and had a strong desire to please. He earned straight As all the way through eighth grade and continued to be an honor student at Sierra High School.

Not only did Jeremy excel academically, but he was also gifted in athletics and very competitive. We always supported him in anything he wanted to try. When he was seven, he asked us if he could run in the Smokey Bear two-mile race in North Fork, California. It was a beautiful fall morning as runners of all ages lined up to start the race.

The starter's gun fired, and they were off. We waited at the finish line, ready to cheer for our son, no matter what position he finished in. To our surprise, as the first group of runners rounded the bend, Jeremy was right up front with them! He was a natural-born runner and continued to run competitively into high school. He also swam competitively, and played baseball, football, and tennis. When he was a freshman, he made the varsity tennis team at Sierra High. I wondered what athletic opportunities he would have at his new school in Missouri.

As I continued to drive east on Interstate 40, I thought about an incident that had happened when Jeremy was twelve years old. There was a misunderstanding when he was playing outside with some neighbor kids, and their mother yelled at him for something that was not his fault. He yelled back at her, and she told him to stay away from her house. Jim and I were out for our evening walk when Jeremy rode up on his bicycle. He told us what had happened, and it was obvious he was really bothered. We told him to ignore her and play somewhere else. He rode off to think some more. When we got home, he told us he had gone back to the neighbor's house and knocked on the door. When the mother answered, he said he was sorry he had yelled at her. She told him she shouldn't have wrongly accused him and that she was sorry too. I was very proud of Jeremy for taking the initiative to make things right. He was a very sensitive young man and did not want to hurt anyone.

I looked over at Jeremy sleeping in the passenger seat beside me. He had grown up to be a very good-looking young man with piercing blue eyes, curly brown hair, and an endearing smile. I wondered what the future would hold for him as we made this move to Missouri and he continued through his teenage years. I had high hopes and great expectations for him.

Jeremy at Pacific Ocean

Chapter 13

—— ❧ ——

Getting Re-established

The drive to Missouri was mostly incident-free, except when we got stranded in a snowstorm in Williams, Arizona. We had to sneak the birds into our motel room under a pile of blankets and hope they didn't start chirping. I had a horrible migraine from lack of sleep, stress, and emotional overload.

The next morning, the weather was still bad, and several feet of snow had fallen overnight. We had snow chains for our tires because we had been living in the mountains. Jeremy tried to put them on but had no success. Finally, we found an open gas station, and they lifted the car up on a rack and put the chains on for us. We slowly continued on our way.

We didn't know it then, but at the same time Jeremy and I were fighting our way through the snowstorm, Jim and Julie were caught in a major flood. Because our furniture had yet to arrive in Van Buren, Jim and Julie were staying on the second floor of a motel along the Current River. After an intense night of rainfall, the river had flooded the first floor of the motel and into much of the town. Jim began to wonder what he had gotten his family into.

After we finally arrived in Van Buren, I enrolled Jeremy in school. Julie had already started and was in class when a girl came into the room after running an errand to the front office. As she walked through the door, she said, "You should see the new boy. He is so cute!" All the girls became excited, since it was a small school and new boys didn't enroll very often.

Julie knew better and stated, "Whatever. He's my brother."

We quickly settled into our new life in Van Buren. We got involved with the largest church in town, First Baptist Church. Jeremy turned sixteen and wanted to buy a truck, so he got a job pumping gas at Phillips 66. Because he often worked on Sundays, he didn't get to attend church on a regular basis. Julie had made a lot of friends and kept busy with church activities. Following one of the events, she decided to be baptized. She wanted everyone to know that an inner change had taken place in her when she had surrendered her life to Jesus Christ years earlier.

One night I was helping her wash her hair, and she started asking about what it meant to be a Christian. I told her it was more than just being born into a Christian family like she was, and it was also more than just going to church as she had done since she was a week old. I explained that everyone had to make a personal decision to give their life to Jesus Christ. Julie prayed right there in the kitchen and asked for forgiveness for her sins and told God she wanted to live for Him. Now, at the age of fourteen, she felt it was time to make it public through baptism.

Moving to the Ozarks of Missouri was somewhat of a culture shock for us. After our first year in Van Buren, we bought some property and had a very nice house built on a hillside above the river. We bought the property from local builders and contracted with them to build us the 2,240-square-foot house—on a handshake. This was quite a contrast from the way business was done in California. It was as if we had stepped back in time about twenty years. People didn't lock their doors, and I had to get on to Jeremy for constantly leaving his keys in his truck. He would say, "This isn't California, Mom." And it wasn't uncommon to see a rifle in a pickup in the school parking lot. In California, that would have been cause for a lockdown and SWAT situation. In Missouri, it just meant it was "huntin' season."

Despite the cultural differences, we enjoyed life in this new environment. Jim was busy building an effective fire-management program for the National Park Service. I was offered a permanent position at Ozark National Scenic Riverways and started my federal government career in June of 1994.

Everything seemed to be going well for us in Van Buren. We had a new church family, a beautiful new home, and good jobs.

Chapter 14

———— ❦ ————

Past Meets Present

Jeremy started having a difficult time toward the end of his junior year in high school. Besides the normal growing pains a young man typically has at that age, he was also being pursued by an attractive woman in her twenties. As a young man of seventeen, it was hard for Jeremy to resist her advances.

To make a break from the uncomfortable female situation, Jeremy decided to go to Ada, as he had done most summers when we lived in California. He had a lot of friends at Ada First Baptist Church and was happy to have the opportunity to spend the summer with them once again.

Another issue I sensed Jeremy was struggling with at that time concerned his biological father. I felt he was at the point that he wanted to meet Nick and had a natural desire to know if life might be better if he was with him. Trying to figure out who you are and what you want to do with your life is hard enough for any teenager. As Jeremy approached his final year of high school, he needed to get closure on his past in order to move forward into adulthood.

We hadn't spoken much about Nick and Jeremy's beginnings over the years. I remember when Jeremy was eleven, he got mad at Jim and told him he wasn't his dad anyway. I think he thought better of it, as he never said anything like that again. The other two instances I remember were when he said everything would be perfect if Jim was his biological father, and once, when he was a little older, referring to Jim, he stated, "Dad is my dad."

Just before Jeremy left for Ada for the summer, he and Jim went to Denver with my dad and Laura's husband to attend a Promise Keepers conference. I knew through mutual friends that Nick had married and now owned a business in a town a few hours from Denver. I asked Jeremy if he would like to meet Nick when he was in Colorado. He said he would think about it and left the house. He came back forty-five minutes later, and as he walked past me, he said, "Yes." I knew what he meant.

I called my friends and got Nick's phone number. Then I prepared to make one of the hardest phone calls I have ever made. I took a deep breath and with a shaky hand dialed his number. The phone rang three or four times before a woman answered. I thought that it must be his wife and contemplated hanging up. Instead, I heard myself ask if Nick was there. She said he was but that he was comforting their three-year-old son who had just cut his lip on the coffee table. (I thought back to when Jeremy had done that when he was a toddler, but Nick wasn't there to comfort him.) "It's business, right?" she said.

"No," I said.

Then she said softly, "Just a moment. I will have him take the call in the other room."

After what seemed like an eternity, Nick picked up the phone and said, "Hello?"

"You'll have to think back about seventeen years," I said. I then went on to tell him who I was. I could literally hear him take a very big gulp. I explained that Jeremy was going to be in Denver in a few weeks and wanted to meet him. He said it would disrupt his schedule, but he would try to make the time. He asked why Jeremy wanted to see him, and I told him he was curious about his biological father. At the end of the conversation, Nick asked me my maiden name. He didn't even remember.

When the appointed time came for them to meet in Denver, Nick wasn't there. The group Jeremy was with could only wait a short time if they wanted to make the Promise Keepers meeting that night. Finally, minutes before they had to go or miss the start of the meeting, Nick drove up in his SUV. Jeremy walked over to meet his biological father by himself. Jim felt it would be best not to interfere, and he let Jeremy do this alone. Nick and Jeremy took a short walk, talked a little, and Jeremy showed Nick some of his sports pictures. That was it. Jim said Jeremy was very quiet for the rest of the trip. I didn't have a chance to ask Jeremy much about it, because he went straight from Denver to Ada. Jeremy did tell me Nick had seen Jim across the parking lot and asked him if that was his dad. Jeremy also shared with me what bothered him most was that Nick had never even told his other biological children that they had a half-brother. Jeremy never mentioned Nick or asked to see him again. Maybe meeting Nick helped him move on and receive some sort of closure.

Chapter 15

---- ❦ ----

Changes for Everyone

After Jeremy arrived in Ada, he got a summer job. He attended First Baptist Church and began dating a girl named Shelley, whom he met in the youth group. When summer ended and it came time for his senior year, he decided to stay and enroll at Ada High School so he could be with Shelley and some of his other friends. I wasn't expecting my son to leave home so soon, but it seemed to be the best thing at the time.

Jeremy graduated from high school in 1996 and then stayed in Ada to attend college at East Central University (ECU) as an English major. However, his first year of college wasn't very successful, because he tended to sleep in and consequently missed a lot of his classes. He ended up dropping half of the classes I had paid for and finished the year with twelve credit hours. I informed him that I wasn't going to pay for any more college if he was going to continue wasting money on classes that he was not attending. Instead of college, I suggested that he learn a skill at a vocational school. Jeremy insisted he needed a college education, so I told him he would have to figure out how to pay for it. After doing some research on military educational benefits, Jeremy joined the Oklahoma Air National Guard. He had always wanted to be a pilot, and this seemed like a win-win situation for him. Jeremy left for basic training in December 1997.

As Jeremy was going into the Air National Guard, we were in the midst of relocating to Roswell, New Mexico. Jim had accepted a position as fire-management officer with the Bureau of Land Management (BLM). I also continued my federal career with BLM for a year before transferring to the US Fish and Wildlife Service. Julie was a junior in high school when we moved to Roswell.

Once Jeremy finished his basic and technical training at Lackland Air Force Base, he moved back to Ada to resume his education at ECU. This time, his blood, sweat, and tears were paying for it. He would spend one weekend a month at the Will Rogers Air National Guard Base in Oklahoma City. He had trained to be an air cargo loader, so he could work with the pilots. His goal was to obtain a college degree so he could go into the air force full time as an officer and then become a pilot. Jeremy finally seemed to be maturing and moving past some of the drama of his teenage years as he settled back into college life.

Jeremy in his Air Force Dress Blues with his
Aunt Sarah in Ada, Oklahoma 1998

Chapter 16

Back on Track

In the spring of 1999, Jeremy met Abby in one of his classes at ECU. Abby was a strikingly beautiful unwed mother with a baby boy. Jeremy started going to her apartment and helping her with her homework. Each day when Jeremy called me, he talked about Abby and her little boy. This went on for a couple of months, and then the relationship seemed to end suddenly. After that, he mentioned Abby from time to time. One day, he told me that he sent her a card, and she had not responded. He said when he saw Abby at school, he felt like he had a big knot in his stomach. I never asked him why the relationship had ended. I assumed she just wasn't that interested in him for some reason.

In the fall of 1999, Jeremy started dating the reigning ECU homecoming queen and seemed to be moving past Abby. He got his own second-story apartment next to campus, so he wouldn't have to get up as early for classes. Then he broke up with the homecoming queen and started seeing Courtney. He had met Courtney hanging around the ECU Baptist Student Union and soon realized they had attended Falls Creek Christian Camp together during high school. Courtney was a cute and petite blond cheerleader with a bubbly personality, and he told me that he loved talking to her.

Jeremy came to see us in Roswell three times that fall, even though it was a nine-hour drive from Ada. He came home in October for a weekend visit and then again for Thanksgiving. Just before Christmas, he came home to move some furniture back to Ada for his new apartment. My sisters, Jeanene and Laura, were on Christmas break and came with Jeremy.

On Monday, December 20, we rented a U-Haul trailer and loaded it with furniture, including a new couch and love seat Jeremy had purchased the last time he was in Roswell. We stood in the driveway and said our good-byes early Tuesday morning as they prepared to depart. I told Jeremy I loved him and told him to be careful. Then I hugged him. Jim and I watched from the garage as they drove away in Jeremy's Eddie Bauer Ford Explorer 4 x 4 with trailer in tow.

They made it home with no mishaps, and Jeremy started making his new apartment comfortable. Jeanene gave Jeremy a hundred-gallon fish tank for his living room. He bought some goldfish, white rocks, and some small clear Christmas lights to put inside the tank. Jeremy's friends told him he was going to get electrocuted trying to put lights inside water. The lights were apparently waterproof, and he didn't even get shocked while setting up the tank. In no time at all, he had his apartment looking just the way he wanted it.

The last week in December, Jeremy drove four hours to Ozark to spend a few days with Jeanene and Laura's families while everyone was still on break for the holidays. They all had a good time together.

Jeremy drove back to Ada via Interstate 40. He was traveling in the left lane at seventy miles an hour when suddenly a vehicle veered toward him from the right lane, forcing him onto the center divider. He eventually came to a complete stop and then sat there until he felt composed enough to continue. He drove until he came to the first phone booth he could find and called to tell me about the incident. He was still quite shaken up as he realized just how close he had come to being killed that day.

Chapter 17

———————— ❧ ————————

When You Least Expect It

Y2K came and went without any of the predicted world-changing events taking place, and the new year was off to a quiet start for our family. During the second week of January, Jim and I were both attending training courses in Albuquerque, two hundred miles northwest of Roswell. Karin, my co-worker at Bitter Lake National Wildlife Refuge, attended the class with me. Our training was scheduled to end at noon on Friday. Jim's class ended earlier in the week, and he returned to Roswell on Thursday morning.

On Thursday evening, Karin and I decided to eat at TGI Friday's and then go shopping. Following class, I returned to my room to change before going out. I noticed the message light was flashing on the hotel phone. It didn't surprise me that it was a message from Jeremy, since he called me at least once every day. I knew I might not have time to talk to him later, so I called him before we left for the restaurant.

He was in a great mood that evening and as we talked he told me he might have a summer job in Tulsa, working as an insurance adjuster. He said he thought he could make some good money. He also told me he was going to the ECU registrar's office the next day to switch his evening science class to a daytime class. He decided this because one of his friends was in the daytime class and so was Abby. I said that sounded good and didn't give it much more thought.

I had planned to talk to him about finances that night. I wanted to remind him that he needed to take more financial responsibility for himself, since his dad would be retiring in less than two years and we would have to cut back. I briefly mentioned to him to be careful with money but didn't give the speech I had intended. As we hung up, I told him I loved him, and he said, "I love you, Mom. Tell Dad and Julie 'hi' when you see them."

Karin and I went out to eat and then did some shopping as planned. I wasn't very hungry, so I took my half-eaten hamburger back to the hotel refrigerator. I thought I would eat it for lunch before checking out the next day. I packed everything except what I needed for the next morning, read my Bible, and spent some time praying before I drifted off to sleep.

The next thing I remember was being awakened by the phone at 6 a.m. I was sound asleep and literally jumped out of bed. At first, I thought it was the alarm. Then I realized that it was the telephone, and I picked it up. It was Jim.

Before I had time to wonder why he would be calling me at that time of the morning, he said, "I have some bad news—some really bad news. Jeremy is dead."

Shock set in immediately, and I responded, "It isn't real. It isn't real."

He said, "I'm afraid it is real, and this is what I want you to do: Call Karin's room and tell her you need to get ready and check out of the hotel. Then you need to meet Julie and me at Clines Corners. We are packed and will be leaving in a few minutes. We will meet you at the Shell gas station at Clines Corners. Now tell me what you are going to do."

I said, "I am going to call Karin's room and tell her she has to take me to Clines Corners and meet you and Julie."

He said, "That's right."

I didn't even ask him how Jeremy died. To me, it didn't matter. My son was apparently dead, and no matter how it happened, he would still be dead. I assumed he had been in a car accident. But just before he hung up, Jim told me, "They say it was suicide."

I was in shock. My mind kept repeating that it just wasn't real. It couldn't be real. I spoke to him only hours ago, and he was in a good mood, making plans for the future. Nothing in our conversation or in his behavior indicated that he would ever do such a thing. I reasoned that he must have been angry about something and accidentally crashed his vehicle.

I called Karin's room, and in a very shaky voice, near tears, I said, "I need you." Her room was across the hall, and she came right over. When I told her that my son had died, she didn't know what to say or do. Karin was expecting her third child, and I was sorry that she had to be put in this situation just because she happened to be with me that week. She told me she would get dressed and be ready in a few minutes. I explained that Jim and Julie had just left Roswell and we were much closer to Clines Corner, so I had time to take a shower and wash my hair as usual. I would call her room when I was ready to go.

Karin left my room, and I mechanically got into the shower and turned the water on. I still didn't fully comprehend the impact of the words Jim had spoken to me moments ago. There had to be some kind of mistake. I couldn't wrap my mind around it. It didn't make sense. I finally started to cry softly as I went through my normal routine.

I called Karin's room to let her know I was almost ready. She told me she would go check out for us and wait for me in the lobby. I gathered my things and walked down the hall to the elevator. I never gave the hamburger I had planned to eat for lunch that day a second thought. I guess the maid found it in the refrigerator when she cleaned the room later that day.

When the elevator doors opened, three young men made room for me to get in. As we started down, I looked at them and said, "I just found out my son died last night. Hug your mothers when you see them." They nodded but didn't say anything back. What could they say? I'm not sure what compelled me to speak to them, but I bet they still remember the encounter.

Karin was waiting for me when I got off the elevator and stepped into the lobby. She wondered how we could reach the teacher from our class, to tell him we had to leave unexpectedly. It was too early for the classroom to be open, so I suggested she write a note and put it on the door. The desk clerk gave her some paper and tape. Karin wrote the note and took it next door to the classroom while I waited in the car. I found out later that all she said on the note was that we had an emergency. The class members thought Karin had some complication with her pregnancy.

Karin came back to the car and handed me a box of Kleenex that the desk clerk had given her. We drove along in the stillness of the early morning as I cried softly and silently prayed. My prayer was for strength to make it through. As I gazed out the car window, I saw a rainbow shining through the clouds. I knew God had placed it there just for me that morning. I remembered the promise that came with the very first rainbow God created.

The book of Genesis tells us that because of all man's wickedness, God decided to destroy everything He had created by flooding the Earth. However, Noah was spared by God because he was the only righteous man. The flood waters came, and Noah, his family, and the animals God told him to take on the ark survived. Once the Earth began to dry out, God made the first rainbow appear in the sky, as a promise that he would never destroy the Earth in a flood again and would be faithful to save anyone who believes and trusts in Him. Even today, a rainbow appears after a storm as a beautiful reminder of God's faithfulness.

On that day, I felt God was saying to me personally that He had not forgotten His promise to me. When I asked Him into my heart, my mom told me He would never leave me. I think the rainbow was there to remind me that He was still there with me. It was a sign of hope and beauty shining out of pain and sadness.

Karin and I arrived at Clines Corner a half hour before Jim and Julie. When they finally pulled into the parking lot, I got out of the car, and we all hugged and cried. Karin said good-bye and headed back to Roswell alone. Julie and I went into the bathroom at the Shell station. I had a great big pain in my heart, and it was strange going into a public place where no one knew what I was feeling. I have often thought about that, especially when I see someone sad or acting out of sorts. You never know what a person may be going through.

While Julie and I were in the bathroom, I said something about Jeremy probably crashing into a tree. I asked her if he was in his SUV. She didn't know what to say, because she thought I knew how he died.

We didn't talk much as we drove east on Interstate 40. After we had been on the road about an hour, my dad called Jim's cell phone. Jim was the only one who had a cell phone at that time because of his work in fire management. I heard Jim tell my dad that I was doing as well as could be expected. Jim told him where we were and when he thought we might get into Ada. After Jim hung up the phone, he said my dad was making arrangements to have Jeremy buried in an old country cemetery two miles from their house. I said I thought Jeremy would like that.

Finally Jim asked if I wanted to know how Jeremy died. I quietly said, "Yes."

Jim took a deep breath and then said, "He hung himself."

I can't begin to explain the feelings I had at that moment. It was a kind of hurt that felt like someone was kicking me in the stomach over and over and I could barely breathe. For most of the next ten hours, I looked out the window and cried off and on. I would stop crying for a while and then, when I let my mind start to comprehend that he could possibly be gone, I would start crying again. I told Jim I had talked to Jeremy about finances the night before and that must be why he did it. I told him I didn't think I had been very strong about it, but it must have made him feel like he was a burden to us. My heart hurt so much, I didn't think I could bear it.

But no matter how much I was hurting inside, I still had peace within. It is hard to explain how you can have peace in the midst of pain. But I was experiencing it right then and would continue to do so throughout the extremely difficult days to come.

I was, and still am, comforted by the thought of the most important decision Jeremy had ever made in his life—to accept Jesus Christ as his Lord and Savior.

From the time Jeremy was born, I sang a medley of songs to him each night before he went to sleep. I would sing songs such as "Jesus Loves Me," "Jesus Loves the Little Children," and "I Love you, a Bushel and a Peck." As soon as he was able, Jeremy sang along. He loved music and had a natural ability to sing on pitch. I got him a cassette player so he could listen to tapes in his bedroom.

One night, Jeremy was sitting on his bed, listening to a tape of Christian children's songs. I smiled as my son sang along with the familiar "Jesus Loves Me." The next song was "Into My Heart, Lord Jesus."

"Mommy, what does that mean?" he asked.

"It means that God sent His Son Jesus to Earth to show us that He loves us and has a plan for us. It's like in the song 'Jesus Loves Me.' The

Bible says Jesus died on the cross for all of the bad things we have done. We need to ask God to forgive us and ask Him to come into our hearts so we can be His children and live our lives for Him."

"I want to do that!" Jeremy exclaimed. And that is what Jeremy did that night. Just as I had done with my mom at my bedside years earlier, Jeremy prayed and asked Jesus to forgive him for his sins and to come into his heart and life.

Jeremy knew that he had just made a very big decision. "Let's go tell Papa what I did!" he said. I will never forget those words. Even as a young child, Jeremy understood how important it was to accept the gift of forgiveness God was offering him through Jesus Christ.

Thoughts like these gave me comfort and strength as I dealt with the sudden and tragic loss of my son.

It was dark when we drove into Ada. I had been going there since I was a year old, and it felt strange knowing that I was there this time to bury my twenty-one-year-old son. As we got closer to my parents' house, I felt a stronger tightening in my stomach. I wondered how my parents were doing. I knew they had not gotten much sleep the night before.

Chapter 18

———— ❦ ————

Arriving in Ada

When we turned into the driveway, I could see my dad standing alone on the front porch. I got out of the car, and he came toward me. He held me close as we both cried. I knew he was not only hurting over the tragic death of his only grandson but also for me and the pain I was experiencing over the loss of my son.

As we stood there in the cold night air, the first thing my dad told me was that Jeremy had scribbled a note to a girl on a piece of scratch paper just before he died. I couldn't even think of who the girl might be. Then my dad said her name was Abby. I was surprised but later remembered that he had talked about her the night before, when he told me he was going to change science classes. I have to admit that I felt somewhat relieved that Jeremy hadn't taken his life that night because of something I had said. In the same moment, I felt bad for Abby and what she must be going through—if she was even aware of what had happened.

After we went inside the house, my dad told me how he and my mom had received the news of Jeremy's death. He said that a young Ada policeman had called about 4:20 a.m. and asked if he was speaking with Mel Haworth. The policeman gave no indication as to why he was calling. He just said that he had bad news and needed to come out to the house to tell them in person.

After they got out of bed and quickly dressed, my mom told my dad they should pray while they waited. They both got down on their knees, and my dad prayed, "Lord, we know we are going to receive bad news. We do not know what that news is. We know it is beyond our capability to handle without You. We ask that You empower us to cope with it and that Your name be glorified in whatever happens." My dad said that an indescribable peace overcame both of them as they released the upcoming events to God.

When the policeman arrived, he was accompanied by Pastor Bob Bender from their church. The pastor had a son named Zack who was a good friend of Jeremy's. Seeing the pastor made my dad realize that this was extremely serious or that it also involved Zack.

The officer confirmed that my dad was Jeremy's grandfather, and then he said, "Your grandson has taken his own life." My dad said that those words should have pushed him to hysteria, but instead he felt peace as God reminded him, *"It's okay. I have things under control."*

After the pastor and police officer left, my dad had the difficult task of notifying everyone in the family about what had happened. He called all of my sisters before calling us. He knew that I was in Albuquerque but did not know how to reach me. He preferred to tell Jim but wasn't sure if Jim had returned home from Albuquerque or not. He realized if he called our house, Julie might answer. He confessed to me that he dreaded that possibility and did not think he could handle having to tell her. Thankfully, according to God's plan, Jim was home and answered the phone.

My dad told me that he kept "shooting up short prayers" to God over the course of the day. He had specifically asked God to watch over us as we received the news and made our way toward Ada. He said he gave no detailed instructions to God, as he is prone to do, but did make the unusual request to form a bubble of protection around the car as we traveled under stressful conditions. Later, Julie commented that it was as if we were traveling in a bubble all the way to Ada. She didn't even know that is exactly what my dad had prayed.

Chapter 19

———— ❦ ————

I Never Planned for This

On Saturday morning, we went to Criswell Funeral Home to make arrangements. I had never in my life given a moment's thought as to what kind of casket, flowers, obituary, songs, or program I would want for my son's funeral. It never crossed my mind that one of my children might die before I did. Amazingly, as each decision was placed before me, I was able to make my desires known.

I selected a beautiful dark-stained hardwood casket. My dad told me that Jeremy's Air National Guard Unit was planning to attend his funeral and wanted to play "Taps," do a twenty-one-gun salute, and present me with the American flag. To complement the flag, I chose red and white carnations to be placed on top of the casket. I asked my mom if someone could sing and play "Jesus Loves Me" on the guitar for the service. She suggested the youth leader from their church. Then I thought a moment and said, "Do you think we could find the music for 'Into my Heart, Lord Jesus' and have it sung as well?" My mom said she could find it.

After the plans were set, the funeral director asked me if I wanted to see my son. He said he looked really good. I had already told my dad I didn't want to see Jeremy, because when I saw my granddad after he died, it didn't look anything like him. To this day, that's how I picture him. Because I didn't want to remember my son like that, I asked for a closed casket. So we left the funeral home without viewing Jeremy's body.

I told my dad I wanted to go to Jeremy's apartment. He was reluctant to let me, but I insisted. He gave us the key, and Jim and I drove to the edge of the East Central University campus to Jeremy's apartment. As we pulled up to the building, I could see the police tape below the balcony where Jeremy had died. We slowly climbed the stairs and entered his apartment. It was the first time I had seen the apartment that Jeremy had told me so much about. To the left was the hundred-gallon aquarium, with several goldfish swimming happily about. The Christmas lights were still plugged in. Straight ahead was his new green couch and loveseat. The end tables I bought him were situated on either side of the couch. He even had a box of Kleenex on one of the tables. Leaning against the wall to the right, Jeremy had a cork bulletin board filled with pictures of his friends. He hadn't had a chance to hang it on the wall.

As I entered the bathroom and looked over at the vanity, I saw the puka-shell necklace Jeremy always wore. I walked out of the bathroom toward his bedroom. There was a basket of dirty clothes on top of the washing machine that was located between his bathroom and bedroom. A green T-shirt, which I later found out Jeremy had worn that night, was in the basket. I picked it up and held it close. It still smelled like his cologne. Next I walked into his bedroom, and at the foot of his waterbed was another laundry basket with his Air National Guard gear in it. The previous weekend, he had been in Oklahoma City for his monthly Guard duty. I remembered that he had told me he had cleaned out his Explorer for a date with his new girlfriend, Courtney. He had apparently taken all of his Guard supplies out of the vehicle and put them in the basket.

As I looked at his waterbed, I recalled something he told me a couple of weeks earlier. When he was moving in, he carried each of the water-filled bladders up the stairs to his apartment all by himself. He said he didn't want to empty them and then have to refill them again. Even though he was pretty buff, it was a great task to carry them over his shoulders and up the stairs without any help.

Several of Jeremy's friends arrived while we were still in his apartment. I started to piece things together as I spoke to them about the events leading up to Jeremy's death. After hanging up from our conversation, Jeremy had called his aunt Sarah. She said he sounded like he was in a good mood and told her he still wanted to take her out to lunch for her twenty-second birthday.

The friends who were with him that night also told us he was in a great mood and in his typical life-of-the-party mode. He and his friends went to dinner at Polo's and then to a club that was a popular local hangout for college students. He had several drinks with dinner before going to the club. We don't drink, and Jeremy knew we didn't approve of him drinking either. But it seemed apparent that he had planned to drink that night, because he didn't drive his own vehicle.

At some point in the evening, Abby arrived at the club with another guy. Jeremy went over to speak to them. Jeremy's friends said his mood visibly changed after this encounter. They could not bring him out of his depressed and angry state, and he continued to drink. One of his friends shared with me that Abby had told Jeremy she and the guy she was with had just gotten engaged.

Some of Jeremy's friends drove him back to his apartment and dropped him off at 1:50 a.m. Around 2 a.m., another friend was let off in the apartment's parking lot to pick up his vehicle. As he walked around the corner to the front of the building, he saw Jeremy hanging from the balcony outside of his apartment.

It appeared that when Jeremy returned to his apartment, he was still very hurt and angry. The alcohol had only fueled the anger and clouded his judgment. I believe he went into his apartment and entered the bathroom to get ready for bed. He probably even brushed his teeth. He took off his necklace and then the T-shirt, which he dropped into the laundry basket as he walked past the washer and dryer. As he walked into his bedroom, he probably noticed the basket with his Guard gear in it. The basket contained some cord that he used when he packed parachutes. He probably remembered in training that they were told how strong the cord was and that it could strangle someone if it got wound around their neck. In his hurt and anger, under the influence of alcohol, and without considering any consequences, Jeremy scribbled the note to Abby and proceeded to take his own life. I was told that he died instantly.

It's hard to believe that I was sleeping soundly 625 miles away from my son when he died. I have heard of instances when people have been awakened from a deep sleep and have felt the urge to pray for a loved one. Later they find out their loved one was in danger at that very moment but miraculously escaped. That didn't happen to me on January 14, 2000.

The Bible says that there is a certain day God appoints one to die (Hebrews 9:27). This was Jeremy's day. I know God could have intervened and stopped it from happening. I believe that when Jeremy put the cord around his neck and jumped off the balcony, Satan was thinking he had won. Unlike God, Satan does not know our hearts. Jeremy had given his heart to God, even though his outward actions over the last couple of years had not always been those of a committed Christian. He had discussed his inner turmoil with me and with others. He said he knew he needed to change some things in his life and start living for God. His struggle reminds me of the following passage in the Bible: "I don't understand myself at all, for I really want to do what is right, but I don't do it. Instead, I do the very thing I hate. I know perfectly well that what I am doing is wrong, and my bad conscience shows that I agree that the law is good. But I can't help myself because it is sin inside of me that makes me do these evil things" (Romans 7:15-17 NLT).

Two weeks before Jeremy died, we attended a New Year's Eve service at our church. We were encouraged to write down prayer requests on special cards that would be placed in the prayer room. People would come and take turns spending time in prayer for the needs of the congregation. I wrote on the card that I would like prayer for my son. I said I knew he was saved, but I would like him to fully surrender every area of his life to God. I knew that Jeremy was struggling with things like drinking. That night as I prayed, I visualized lifting Jeremy up toward heaven with my outstretched arms. It was my desire that Jeremy live the life God had intended for him.

After Jeremy died, I realized that God had indeed answered my prayer request. He was as totally and fully surrendered as anyone can be. Jeremy was in the presence of the one true and living God. The prayer wasn't answered in the way I would have thought, but it was indeed answered.

Chapter 20

❦

God Grieves with Us

Saturday evening, Pastor Bob Bender and his wife, Beverly, came out to the house to talk about the funeral, which was scheduled for Monday morning. Their son Zack had arranged for some of Jeremy's friends to be the pall bearers for the funeral.

We told the pastor that we wanted to have Jeremy's testimony read at the service. It was our desire to make sure everyone in attendance heard the hope that is offered in Jesus Christ. The main thing we wanted was for God to be glorified for who He is and for all He has done for us. They prayed with us, and before they left, Beverly said that God would bless us for wanting to glorify Him through this tragedy.

Jim and I slept restlessly that night. Around 4 a.m., we were both wide awake. We started talking and praising God for His great love for us and His faithfulness in all situations. We thanked God that one day we would be with our son again. We prayed that through Jeremy's death, others would give their lives to Jesus Christ just as Jeremy had done.

As we prayed in the quiet of the early morning hours, something supernatural happened. It started when Jim asked me if I felt anything strange. I did not. Jim felt a physiological change coming over him. It was as if he were drifting into a different state of being. He told me later he thought he might be dying and everything else ceased to exist except the presence of God. Suddenly, Jim started talking out loud to

God. I heard him say in a choked voice, "You don't have to apologize to me, God." Then again, "You don't have to apologize to me." Jim started to cry and pulled me closer. He asked me once more if I could hear or feel anything. I said I could not. Jim continued to have a dialogue with God in a realm to which I was not privy. While keeping his eyes focused toward the ceiling, Jim said to me in a whispery voice, "God says He is so sorry He had to take our son, but that time is short." At that moment, I realized that God was grieving with us over the earthly loss of our son.

The last thing that happened was that somehow God allowed Jeremy to convey a message to Jim. "Dad, I'm so happy now."

After Jim's encounter with God, he was very weak and couldn't stand up for the next half hour. We feel he came as close to God the Father as any earthly body can.

At breakfast, I told my family about the encounter Jim had with God a few hours earlier. Jim was unable to speak about it without extreme emotion. As I shared what had transpired, my brother-in-law, Darrel, told us about what he had experienced around that same time.

Darrel and Jeanene had been sleeping in the sunroom, which faces the back portion of the property. Darrel said he woke up around 4 a.m. and stepped out the back door instead of going all the way through the house to use the bathroom. As he walked outside into the chill of the winter night, he felt an evil presence all around him. He began to pray that God would overcome the evil that seemed to loom in the darkness. He had a sense that a spiritual battle was taking place in the trees surrounding the perimeter of the house. He quickly went back inside and continued to pray. As soon as Jeanene woke up, he told her about his experience. When I shared what had happened to Jim, Darrel realized that he had witnessed the forces of God and Satan in spiritual conflict as God came to us in great compassion to share our grief. Satan knew that if he could get us to be mad at God or not trust Him through this loss, we would be ineffective in glorifying God. Satan has never been and never will be a match for God, but he still tries to get in the way. God, as always, won the victory that night!

When I get sad and start to dwell on the circumstances of Jeremy's death and our loss, all I have to do is remember that night when God reached His loving arms around us in Ada, Oklahoma, and grieved with us. God, the Creator of the universe, came to us in our loss and gave us peace, hope, and comfort. That is so amazing to me. We immediately realized that this was the blessing Pastor Bender's wife had said we would receive for desiring to glorify God through this storm in our lives.

Zack Bender and Jeremy at their graduation from Ada High School 1996

Chapter 21

———— ❦ ————

Saying Good-bye

Sunday afternoon, Jeremy's friends came back to his apartment and we told them they could take anything of his that they wanted. They mostly chose photographs, and a few took shirts or sweatshirts that would remind them of him.

As I talked to his friends that day, I was amazed at how many of them said Jeremy was their best friend. He was very well liked, and many people looked up to him because he had a way of making everyone feel special. He was one of those people who never met a stranger. I remember one time when he and Sarah came to New Mexico and we took them to Carlsbad Caverns. As we were walking around in the underground caverns, Jeremy saw a guy with a sweatshirt from the University of Oklahoma. He just walked right up to him and started talking about Oklahoma as if he had known the guy all his life. He could always find common ground with people.

That afternoon in Jeremy's apartment, we met the young man who found Jeremy just moments after he died. As we sat on Jeremy's couch, he shared with me that he had been raised in a Christian family. I asked him if he had a personal relationship with Jesus Christ, and he said he did. I hugged him and told him that I was so sorry he had to be the one to find Jeremy but that God must have a special purpose for his life. I assured him I would be praying for him.

On Sunday evening, some members of my family went to the funeral home to say good-bye to Jeremy. I guess they didn't tell us until after the fact because I had said I didn't want to see my son dead but wanted to remember him as alive and vibrant. After the viewing, my dad asked me to reconsider having a closed casket. He said that Jeremy looked very natural and thought it would be good for people to see him one last time. I trusted that he was right and decided to allow an open casket.

The next morning we buried our son. The funeral service was held at Criswell Funeral Home, and the room was overflowing with over 350 people in attendance. The entire English Department from East Central University was there. Jeremy's Air National Guard unit members came from all over Oklahoma and Arkansas. Jeremy's friends from Ada and even about a dozen friends from Van Buren, Missouri, attended the funeral.

The service included the two songs I asked to be sung. Then one of the Air National Guard commanders spoke from his heart about what Jeremy meant to all of them. He broke down as he shared how Jeremy had always been the one to encourage the others to not give up and how his positive attitude was contagious. He said Jeremy always knew how to make them laugh.

As we had requested, the youth pastor presented God's plan of salvation with a clear message of everyone's need of forgiveness for their sins. God had gathered a big audience that day to hear about His grace and forgiveness.

Then Pastor Bender spoke about Jesus and Lazarus (John 11:1–40). He shared how Jesus had openly wept over the death of his dear friend and the pain He saw the family going through.

Lastly, Pastor Bender read Jeremy's testimony of how he had come to give his life to Jesus Christ.

I will never forget exactly how I felt as I sat through my son's funeral. Even with tears streaming down my face, I was smiling because of the peace I had in knowing Jeremy was safe in the arms of our Savior. It is truly a peace that passes understanding. I kept praying during the service that others would open their hearts and surrender to Jesus Christ.

At the end of the service, the casket was slowly and reverently opened, and we watched from a distance as friends passed by and paid their respects. Many tears were shed. One friend slipped a photograph of the two of them into the casket with Jeremy.

Then it was time for the family to pass by. I walked to the front of the room with Jim at my side. I slowly looked down into the casket at my precious son. He looked very peaceful and as if he was smiling. I touched his arm and it felt stiff. I reached up and felt his curly, coarse brown hair. I could not hold back my tears as I bent down and kissed him on his head for the last time. Finally Jim told me it was time to go.

We walked outside the funeral home, and I was amazed to see so many young people. I spoke to as many as I could and thanked them for coming. Courtney found us and introduced herself to me and told me about a two-hour conversation she and Jeremy had had seven days earlier. She said he had told her he needed to change some things in his life. He said he knew he wasn't living the way God wanted him to, and he wanted to change that. Starting a relationship with a good Christian girl like her was a step in the right direction. This sweet girl, who by all rights should be sad and defeated, was joyful as she talked about Jeremy and what she knew about his last days on Earth. She told how Jeremy had opened up to her about so many things. She said he was so proud of his sister and told her Julie was very smart. She wanted us to know that she had no doubt that Jeremy was saved and had gone to be with our Lord when he died. She was such a blessing to us—like an angel sent to bring good news.

Finally we got back into the limo and drove toward the cemetery. A long procession of over a hundred vehicles followed behind us. All other traffic came to a standstill as we headed out of town. I felt like I was in a dream as we traveled down the streets that Jeremy had so often driven over the past few years.

At the cemetery, the funeral continued with the playing of "Taps" and a twenty-one-gun salute by Jeremy's Guard unit. The flag was taken off of the casket, ceremoniously folded, and then presented to me. It was a very emotional experience as the guardsman said, "This flag is presented on behalf of the president of the United States, and a grateful nation, as a token of appreciation for the honorable and faithful service rendered by your loved one."

As the casket was lowered into the ground, I thought back to July 27, 1984 and to what Jeremy said when Sheba died. I knew at that moment, as long as I live on this Earth, that my heart will always cry for Jeremy.

Chapter 22

※

Jesus Loves Me

The day after the funeral, we went to pick out a headstone for Jeremy's grave. We selected a fairly simple granite stone. Other than his name and dates, I hadn't decided what to have inscribed on it. I told the people at the store that I would call later in the week and let them know if I wanted them to add anything.

The following morning, my mom said she knew exactly what we should have inscribed. When she told us we all knew it was perfect. It was simply, *Jesus Loves Me.* As soon as the store opened that day, I called and told them.

On Wednesday morning, Jim and Julie left Ada in Jeremy's Eddie Bauer Ford Explorer and returned to Roswell. I stayed in Ada the rest of the week to finish sorting through Jeremy's things and settle his affairs.

When Jeremy died, he was wearing jeans and his shoes and socks. He had his driver's license, debit card, and six dollars in his pocket. We found his wallet and checkbook in his vehicle. On Wednesday morning, I went to his bank to close out his account, containing a total of $26 and change. The teller told me I was not authorized to have his money and that it would have to go through his estate. I told her that account was all he had. The teller said she knew Jeremy from his visits to the bank and that she had seen his obituary in the *Ada Evening News.* I shared with her that Jeremy was a Christian and had surrendered his life to Jesus Christ at a young age. I told her I missed him very much but knew that I would see him again because of my personal relationship with Jesus Christ as well. She hugged me and told me that when she saw that he had died, she had hoped he was a Christian, and that she had just recently become a believer herself. In the end, she allowed me to sign a form to close out his account.

I spent the rest of Wednesday and Thursday going through Jeremy's things in his apartment. Sarah and her husband Billy took his new couch and loveseat. Other furniture was given to Laura's girls.

On Friday morning, we loaded my dad's pickup with the things I wanted to keep, and prepared for the drive back to Roswell. Just before we headed out, I asked everyone to step outside of Jeremy's apartment so I could be left alone for a few moments. I knew Jeremy was no longer there, but I wanted to stand silently in the place where he had taken his last breath on this Earth.

Finally, we slowly pulled away from Jeremy's apartment building. More tears flooded my eyes as Laura drove me in my car, and her husband followed in my dad's pickup. I was going back to Roswell where I would have to figure out my life without Jeremy.

Chapter 23

———— ❦ ————

This I Know

One of the reasons I wanted to write this book was to share some of the things that I have learned through my son's death. These are things that I am confident about because I have studied them in the Scripture and found them to be true.

I know that God is in control of my life and nothing happens to me that wasn't first filtered through Him. A few weeks before Jeremy died, our pastor, Bobby Renfro, had preached a very powerful sermon on that subject. The words he spoke that Sunday morning immediately came back to us as if God had been preparing us for such a time as this. Pastor Bobby said that no matter how difficult or painful things are, God is still in control.

It can be hard to understand why bad things happen to good people. There is an account in the Bible where Jesus was asked why a certain man had been born blind. Those questioning wondered if the blindness was caused by the man's sins or the sins of his parents. Jesus said that it was neither of their sins. The reason God had allowed the man to be born blind was so that Jesus could heal him that day and thus bring glory to God for the miracle (John 9:1–3). It is my prayer that Jeremy's death continues to bring glory to God and point others to the only true and living God.

I know that I will see Jeremy again one day, because we both personally accepted Jesus Christ's death on the cross as payment for our sins. The Bible tells about King David's son, who became very sick and died. However, David knew he would see his son again:

> David begged God to spare the child. He went without food and lay all night on the bare ground. The elders of his household pleaded with him to get up and eat with them, but he refused. Then on the seventh day the child died. David's advisers were afraid to tell him. "He wouldn't listen to reason while the child was ill," they said. "What drastic thing will he do when we tell him the child is dead?" When David saw them whispering, he realized what had happened. "Is the child dead?" he asked. "Yes," they replied, "he is dead." Then David got up from the ground, washed himself, put on lotions, and changed his clothes. He went to the Tabernacle and worshiped the Lord. After that, he returned to the palace and was served food and ate. His advisers were amazed. "We don't understand you," they told him. "While the child was still living, you wept and refused to eat. But now that the child is dead, you have stopped your mourning and are eating again." David replied, "I fasted and wept while the child was alive, for I said, "Perhaps the Lord will be gracious to me and let the child live. But why should I fast when he is dead? Can I bring him back again? I will go to him one day, but he cannot return to me." (II Samuel 12:16-23 NLT)

I know Jeremy will not come back to me, but I will one day go to him.

I know I can still have peace and joy even though my son is not with me at this time. The Bible says, "Our hearts ache, but we always have joy. We are poor, but we give spiritual riches to others. We own nothing, and yet we have everything" (II Corinthians 6:10 NLT).

I know that "right thinking" rather than destructive thinking is what God wants from me. The Bible says, "And now, dear brothers and sisters, one final thing. Fix your thoughts on what is true, and honorable, and right, and pure, and lovely, and admirable. Think about things that are excellent and worthy of praise" (Philippians 4:8 NLT).

I know that destructive thinking will only lead to depression and make me unable to share with others about God's plan for us. After Jeremy died, I had the choice to dwell on thoughts about how he died and if I could I have done something different that would have prevented him from taking his own life. That kind of thinking only pulls me down and keeps me from the blessings God has for me. Right thinking draws me closer to God as I dwell on all that He has done for me and trust Him to be in control of my life.

I know that if Jeremy had lived to be a hundred years old and been a very rich, famous, kind-hearted person but never accepted God's free gift of salvation, he would be separated from God for eternity. Jeremy had made the most important decision one can make in life. Nothing else matters. All fame, fortune, and charitable donations will fade away, and only what has been settled with our Creator will count for eternity. "And what do you benefit if you gain the whole world but lose your own soul?" (Mark 8:35 NLT).

I know that God sees the big picture, and we cannot understand why He allows some things to happen. One day He will show us how the puzzle pieces all fit together. But for now, I simply have to trust that He knows what is best and He knows what will count eternally. The Bible says that God's ways are not our ways and His thoughts are far above ours (Isaiah 55:8–9). I trust God completely, because He knows all and sees all from a spiritual perspective that I cannot fully understand.

Chapter 24

☿

Suicide

Losing a child is hard enough, but when it is the result of suicide, it takes on a whole new dimension. As a parent, you think that you must have done something wrong in the parenting process. You feel like everyone else is judging you and wondering where you messed up.

There is a stigma that comes with suicide. For some reason, I almost always say that Jeremy took his own life rather than committed suicide. In my mind, it just has a different connotation to it.

Some people believe if you take your own life, you go directly to hell. One of my aunts told me she always thought that and immediately went to talk to her pastor after Jeremy died. He assured her that if a person has been saved, they will go to heaven, no matter how they die.

Calvary Chapel Pastor Chuck Smith addresses this issue in his book, *Answers for Today*. He responds to the question: is a person who commits suicide totally lost for eternity?

"Definitely not! I believe that a person who is driven to the point of committing suicide no longer has responsibility for the things he's doing. Driven to a point of such mental extremes, he isn't necessarily responsible for the action of taking his own life. Certainly, Scripture doesn't indicate anywhere that this is an unpardonable sin. The only sin for which there is no forgiveness is that of rejecting Jesus Christ as your Lord and Savior."

Jeremy had confessed his sins to God and entered into a relationship with Jesus Christ. The Bible says, "If we confess our sins, He is faithful and just to forgive us our sins and to cleanse us from all unrighteousness" (I John 1:9 NLT). God saw Jeremy as right with Him because he had accepted Jesus's death on the cross as payment for his sins. It was only through Jesus he was made right with God. It is as if Jesus is the bridge to God. God is so holy that sinful man is not acceptable to Him. That's why Jesus died and rose again to make a way for us. Jesus put it like this: "I am the way, the truth, and the life. No one can come to the Father except through me" (John 14:6 NLT).

I relate death by suicide to what I shared earlier about myself; I was already saved when I got pregnant with Jeremy. If I had died before asking God to forgive me for that particular sin, I would have still gone to heaven, because at the age of eight I had confessed to God that I was a sinner and I realized He sent His Son Jesus to die for all of my sins—past, present, and future. The consequence of failing to confess my sin of fornication was like when I did something wrong and didn't tell my parents—like the time I lied about how my dress got torn. Until I confessed what I had done, there was a rift in our relationship. As long as I was holding something back, I could not enjoy an open relationship with my parents. However, no matter what I did or will do, they are still my parents. Likewise, no matter what sin a truly born-again believer commits, he is still saved.

Even if I had previously thought (and I did not) that suicide led to hell, I would have thought otherwise because of Jim's encounter with God that night in Ada. God came to us and assured us that Jeremy was with Him. God is so very good!

On several occasions I have told Jim that I can accept God's timing for Jeremy's death. But what I don't understand is why it had to be suicide. Jim told me that because it was suicide, more people paid attention and consequently more lives were touched.

Jim also reminded me of an incident that had greatly impacted his life just a couple of months before Jeremy died. One afternoon, Jim was watching television. He ended up tuning into the funeral service for golf pro Payne Stewart. Stewart had died in a freak accident on

October 25, 1999, when the airplane he was flying in suffered a loss of cabin pressure and everyone on board died. Jim told me that Payne Stewart had become a Christian about three years earlier. He had read that before that time, people who knew him said he could be rude and arrogant. After Payne professed Christ openly and publicly, a lot of people began to notice changes in his attitude and actions. Then he died in a manner that brought a lot of media attention. Because of his recent commitment to Christ, followed by his tragic death, literally thousands of people came to know Christ. Jim said seeing Payne Stewart's funeral on television that day helped him see that God can use tragic events in the lives of Christians to bring glory to Himself. In our case, the added tragedy of it being suicide, gave us a bigger audience to share with others the hope we have in Christ.

Endnotes

1. Used by permission. *Answers For Today* by Chuck Smith, (The Word For Today, Santa Ana, CA, 1993.)

Chapter 25

———— ❦ ————

What Am I Supposed to Do Now?

When the shock of Jeremy's sudden death wore off, I started to feel unbelievable pain, as if a knife was being thrust into my stomach. It was excruciating and almost unbearable. I didn't feel like eating, and I had a continuous sick feeling in the pit of my stomach for weeks. The one thing that helped me with my pain more than anything else was that Jim would hold me and let me cry as long as I needed. No words were necessary. He would simply hold me.

I thought about the missed opportunities to do things with Jeremy. For example, I remembered the weekend we went to San Antonio to watch him graduate from basic training. We headed home early Sunday morning instead of going to church with him like he wanted. I also wish I hadn't cut our phone conversation short the night he died. If I had only known it was the last time I would talk to him on this Earth, I would have stayed on the phone all night.

Jeremy had been gone about eighteen months when I began to feel very sad. I kept telling myself that I knew God was in control and I knew Jeremy was in heaven and I would see him again one day. I couldn't understand what was happening. I decided to go to a Christian counselor. As I talked to the counselor, he assured me that this was normal. I wasn't losing my faith in God. He explained that often around eighteen to twenty-four months after a loved one dies, the loss becomes final. You realize they aren't coming back. What used to be "normal" will never exist again. I finally accepted the fact that when the phone rang, it would never again be my son's voice on the other end.

Finding a "new normal" is even more difficult when it comes to significant days. I want to share some of the things I have done on some significant days since Jeremy's death. I have found there is no right or wrong thing to do. You just have to do what seems right for you and for your healing.

I have stayed home from work every January 14 and every one of Jeremy's birthdays since he died. I feel that if I went to work that day, I would end up telling everyone I spoke with that it would have been my son's birthday or the anniversary of his death. I don't want to put people in an awkward position or make anyone feel uncomfortable, so I choose not to work.

On the first anniversary of his death, I stayed home and compiled a tape of video clips from everything we had taken of him since we got a camcorder when he was five years old. Most years since he died, I have stayed home all day, and a couple of times, I have gone out shopping alone.

On several of Jeremy's birthdays, I have released balloons as a memorial to him. My sisters usually do that from where they live as well. Sometimes we have balloons releasing from California, New Mexico, Oklahoma, and Arkansas on the same day.

March 20, 2004 would have been Jeremy's twenty-sixth birthday. On that day, we gathered outside of the administration building at East Central University in Ada and planted a tree in Jeremy's memory. I had contacted the president of the university, Dr. Cole, and he personally selected the site for the tree to be planted. We often stop by the campus when we are in Ada to see how the tree is doing. It is a beautiful memorial to Jeremy and is growing straight and tall.

On January 14, 2010, I took the day off work and began writing this book. Several years ago, I started to write one but never got past the first page. This time it was different. I am convinced that the timing is perfect and feel now is the time God wants me to share how good and faithful He has been to me throughout my life. Despite my disobedience and mistakes, God has loved me and carried me through and given me the strength to make it. My faith in God has grown as I have seen Him work in miraculous ways and felt His presence through it all. It is my desire that what I have experienced in my life and shared in these pages will bring encouragement and hope to others.

Chapter 26

—— ❦ ——

Hope for Others

After Jeremy died, I found a wide-open audience of people who would listen to me. I felt like I had to tell people that my son had died. Not a single person ever told me they would rather not hear about it. I told the clerk at the post office, store cashiers, or someone sitting next to me in the waiting room at the doctor's office. I always shared with them that I was not without hope, because Jeremy had a personal relationship with Jesus Christ, so I would see him again in heaven one day. If the person was a born-again Christian, they understood. If they were not, they would just smile and nod politely.

A few months after Jeremy died, people started contacting me to ask if I would call, visit, or e-mail someone they knew who had just lost a child. I was always willing to do so because I was eager to share God's love and faithfulness. I did have one problem: if the person did not know if their loved one had made a personal decision to surrender their life to Jesus Christ before they had died, I simply did not know what to say to them. I didn't want to give them a false hope in saying that everyone who dies goes to heaven. I didn't even want them to think that just because their loved one was a good and kind person, they would go to heaven. I prayed for God to give me something to say in times like this.

God orchestrated a chain of events that answered my prayer. The week Jeremy died, I read my first Max Lucado book, *No Wonder They Call Him the Savior*. Max Lucado writes inspirational, encouraging books designed to draw the reader closer to God. I loved Max Lucado's writing style, so I bought more of his books and soaked in the encouraging words. In 2001, Max Lucado wrote a book about the Twenty-third Psalm called *Traveling Light*. The entire book is wonderful, but an answer to my question came in chapter 11 entitled, "When Mourning Comes." This is what it says:

Who among us is privy to a person's final thoughts? Who among us knows what transpires in those final moments? Are you sure no prayer was offered? Eternity can bend the proudest knees. Could a person stare in to the yawning canyon of death without whispering a plea for mercy? And could our God, who is partial to the humble, resist it?

He couldn't on Calvary. The confession of the thief on the cross was both a first and final one. But Christ heard it. Christ received it. Maybe you never heard your loved one confess Christ, but who is to say Christ didn't?

We don't know the final thoughts of a dying soul, but we know this. We know our God is a good God. He is "not willing that any should perish but that all should come to repentance" (2 Peter 3:9). He wants your loved one in heaven more than you do.

When I read those words, I starting thinking that because God is so fair and just, He may come to someone He knows will die soon and give them one last chance. As if to say, "Is that your final answer?"

Since I read that book, I have given copies of it to many hurting people. The way Max Lucado presents this topic makes sense to me. After all, when it comes right down to it, no one but God knows our hearts. No one but God knows our final thoughts. The truth is, everyone has the same opportunity to either accept or reject what Jesus Christ has already done for us on the cross. The opportunity is there up until the moment we take our final breath. I am certain that no one will be able to stand before God at the final judgment and say that He never showed them the way to salvation at some point during their life. "They know the truth about God because he has made it obvious to them.

For ever since the world was created, people have seen the earth and sky. Through everything God made, they can clearly see his invisible qualities—his eternal power and divine nature. So they have no excuse for not knowing God" (Romans 1:19–20 NLT).

It is far better to accept Jesus Christ as soon as you realize that you are a sinner in need of a Savior and not to count on a last-minute opportunity. Eternity is forever, and I wouldn't want to put off securing my final destination. Also, I can't imagine facing life without knowing God.

Endnotes

2. Reprinted by permission. *Traveling Light: Releasing the Burdens You Were Never Intended to Bear,* Max Lucado, 2001, Thomas Nelson Inc. Nashville, Tennessee. All Rights reserved.

Chapter 27

— ❦ —

What Happened to the Other Players?

People often ask me how Nick is dealing with Jeremy's death. I honestly don't know. We had not been in contact with him since Jeremy met him in Denver. After Jeremy died, I sent Nick a very short note in which I enclosed a copy of the e-mail my dad had sent out right after Jeremy died. It said something like this:

> On January 14th, his heart broken by the rejection of a girl he cared for deeply, and his mind clouded by the use of excessive alcohol Jeremy took his own life. It was spontaneous; no one could have possibly foreseen it. Conversations with his friends and family earlier in the evening gave no indication of Satan's impending attack.

At the top of the page I wrote, "I thought you should know about this."

A few years after Jeremy died, I wrote a long letter to Nick, telling him all about Jeremy's life. At the end of the letter, I told him I wouldn't contact him ever again. If he received the letters, he did not acknowledge them.

People also want to know how the young man who found Jeremy that night is doing. I know God has worked in his life in incredible ways over the years, and recent contact with him indicates that he is doing okay. So many of Jeremy's friends were affected by what Jeremy did that night—but none so much as this young man, who has had to live with the memory of what he encountered when he innocently arrived at Jeremy's apartment building in the early hours of January 14, 2000.

Another person I am asked about is Abby. Abby never saw the note Jeremy wrote to her that night. (I didn't even see it until three months after his death.) It appears to start with a poem or words to a song that he may have written. This is exactly what he wrote:

Don't hold it against me
and don't call me scared!
I am lost in love's deep trenches
I'm lost in despair
You can't feel me
My pain
My sorrow
I can hide it like a clown
You be happy
f--- your sad
I am better now
Abby!!!!!

I never met Abby, although I understand that she and her fiancé were at the funeral. The day after I left Ada, she went out to my parents' house to deliver a letter she had written to the family. My mom held Abby in her arms as tears of pain, regret, and sadness overcame her.

In the letter, she asked us to forgive her for being selfish and for ignoring Jeremy when he kept reaching out to her. She thanked us for raising a godly, loving, and gentle man and said she was blessed to have known him. She knew without a doubt Jeremy loved God. She said she knew God, and one day when she saw Jeremy again, she would be able to ask his forgiveness. Until that day, she would never forget the young man who loved her regardless of what she said or did.

After I received the letter, I wrote back to Abby. I made sure she knew that we did not blame anyone for his death, and there was nothing any of us could have done to prevent it. Even though Jeremy's heart was broken by the news he received that night, the biggest contributor to his death was excessive use of alcohol. I told her I knew God was in control and assured her of the hope we have in knowing we will see Jeremy again. That is the last contact we have had with her, but I still pray for her and her son.

I have read that it is very common for people to want to blame someone for their loss. It is all part of trying to make sense of something that just doesn't make sense. The blame can be directed toward God. It can be directed toward the person who died. Or it can be directed at the one who may actually be responsible for the death, such as a drunk driver. In my case, it could have been directed at Abby, but I don't blame her. I feel certain it is because I knew from the start that God could have intervened and stopped this from happening if He chose to do so. God sees the big picture and knew that Jeremy's death would bring others to salvation. I can say truthfully from my heart that if Jeremy's death meant that even one person would be saved as a result, it was worth it. It's all about eternity and our final destination.

Chapter 28

————————— ❦ —————————

He Keeps on Blessing

Jeremy had been gone eighteen months when Jim decided to go through some things in our storage shed. It was during the time I was seeing a counselor. In God's perfect timing, Jim found a journal Jeremy had written in while attending a Super Summer Christian camp at Oklahoma Baptist University when he was fifteen. The focus of the week was to encourage Christian youth to share with others what God had done in their lives. This is what Jeremy wrote in his journal:

> Dear God,
>
> I love you. I thank you for showing me that I have a purpose in life. I thank you for showing me I need to do more than just be a Christian, but to help lead others to you. The handshake five thing tonight really had an impact on me tonight. When Buddy winked at me I knew that I would do something major for you someday. When I grow up aside from being a pilot I want to be a youth minister. With your help Lord I know I can. The 'life for a life' really hit me. You spoke to me and told me that Jesus gave his life for me so I must give mine for not just <u>one</u>, but <u>many</u>. Lord, the people here are great. I want to come next year, and I pray that if I do you'll give people who will

touch my life as much as Aaron, Stephany, Buddy, Bill, and Lou. Heavenly Father <u>thank you</u> for letting me come to S.S. this week and bring <u>me</u> closer to you. Please help me to stay on my Spiritual high after this week and help me with the temptations the devil might try to tempt me with. I love you. Thank you, Jeremy

That discovery was such an encouragement and blessing to us. God knew just when I needed it most. God is so good.

In November of 2008, Julie bought me a picture frame with this inscription:

> *Faith...*
> *Now faith is being sure of what we hope for*
> *and certain of what we do not see.*
>
> *Hebrews 11:1*

When Julie gave it to me, I said that I wished I had a more recent picture of Jeremy to put in it. I immediately realized what I had said would be impossible.

Then, on December 25, 2008, I received the best Christmas present ever. As I opened my present from Julie, I saw a black photo album. When I turned to the first page, I saw an unfamiliar picture of Jeremy. As I flipped page after page, every picture was unfamiliar. I couldn't contain my tears as I said, "I've never seen these pictures before!" Then Julie proceeded to tell me the whole amazing story.

A few mornings after she gave me the picture frame, Julie was walking through the kitchen and happened to glance at Jeremy's senior picture hanging on the refrigerator. She said it was as if Jeremy was looking right at her. Since he had graduated from Ada High School and had his senior pictures taken in Ada, my involvement was limited to payment for the two poses he chose. For all I knew, those were the only two poses that turned out decent. As Julie looked at the picture that morning, she wondered if he had other poses taken and if so maybe the proofs still existed. She wasn't discouraged by the fact that it had been thirteen years since the photo shoot.

Julie found the photography studio that had taken the photos on the Internet and sent an e-mail on the off chance they still had his proofs. A few hours later, she received a reply that they had sixteen photos in an old file. Julie bought them sight unseen. At that point, it didn't matter if they were very good or not. What was important was that they had additional photos we had never seen.

The photos arrived just days before Christmas. To Julie's delight, the photos were all good. She couldn't wait for me to open this amazing gift. God is so good.

Chapter 29

--- ❦ ---

The Hope of Heaven

"For everyone has sinned; we all fall short of God's glorious standard. Yet God, with undeserved kindness, declares that we are righteous. He did this through Christ Jesus when he freed us from the penalty for our sins. For God presented Jesus as the sacrifice for sin. People are made right with God when they believe that Jesus sacrificed his life, shedding his blood. God did this to demonstrate his righteousness, for he himself is fair and just, and he declares sinners to be right in his sight when they believe in Jesus" (Romans 3:23–26 NLT).

Only those who surrender to Jesus Christ are made right with God and will spend eternity in heaven with Him.

I have thought a lot about heaven since Jeremy died. I know God created us to have and enjoy relationships on this Earth and also into eternity. The greatest relationship we can have is with Jesus Christ. In heaven, we will not only be forever with the Lord, but we will continue to have relationships with our loved ones and friends who have also put their faith and trust in God.

Jeremy has gone on before us to our eternal home. Jesus said, "There are many rooms in my Father's home, and I am going to prepare a place for you. If that were not so, I would tell you plainly. When everything is ready I will come and get you, so that you will always be with me where I am" (John 14:2–3 NLT).

Soon after Jeremy died, Jim had a dream. In the dream, he was standing in the kitchen and he looked up and saw Jeremy walk into the room. Jim asked, "Jeremy, where have you been?"

Jeremy replied, "No, Dad. Where have *you* been?"

I wake up each day knowing that I am one day closer to heaven than I was the day before. I cling to God's promise: "He will wipe every tear from their eyes, and there will be no more death or sorrow or crying or pain. All these things are gone forever. And the one sitting on the throne said, 'Look, I am making everything new!' And then he said to me, 'Write this down, for what I tell you is trustworthy and true'" (Revelation 21:4–5 NLT).

Knowing that Jeremy is in heaven right now is one of my greatest joys. I can't wait to see him again. I can imagine the moment I step into eternity and see my Savior with His arms open wide. I think in the next moment, I will see my son again. Jeremy will have a great big smile on his face. It is only because of what God has done for us that we have this sure hope and promise of eternal life with Him. I can't wait for the day I arrive in heaven and *my heart will no longer cry.*

Uncle Darrel, Jeremy and Aunt Jeanene - December 26, 1999

Resources:

Website: *www.mightbetoday.com/heart*

References:

1. Lucado, Max. *Traveling Light: Releasing the Burdens You Were Never Intended to Bear* (Nashville, Tenn.: Thomas Nelson, Inc., 2001), 92–93.

2. Smith, Chuck. *Answers for Today* (Costa Mesa, Calif.: The Word for Today, 1993), 116.

CPSIA information can be obtained at www.ICGtesting.com
226295LV00005B/3/P

9 781449 716042